Rear View Mirror

"The Confessions of a Sinner"
BASED ON A TRUE STORY

KENESA BOWE

SpeakLife Publishing

ISBN: 978-0692294826
SpeakLife Publishing

DEDICATION

This book is dedicated to the readers & my children; Kemarri, Khyleed & Ka'Ryzma. Thank you for believing in me and know that with God all things are possible. I love you all very much!

CONTENTS

ACKNOWLEDGMENTS

I would like to thank the many people who have made this book possible:

First I would like to thank my spiritual parents, Apostle William K. Moore & Prophetess Dorothy O. Moore. Thank you for your teachings, believing in me and nurturing me to be who God called me to be. Your selflessness will be remembered always. I love you both very much. Thank you "Doors of Faith."- my church family.

To my parents, for raising me in a Christian home & exposing me to Christ. Proverbs 22:6 says, "Train up a child in the way she should go, And when she is old she will not depart from it." Thank you & I love you both.

To my sisters, for always being there for me when I needed you to be. The bond that we share is unbreakable. I thank all of you because you all have inspired my life in many ways. I love you to life ladies.

To my children, Kemarri, Khyleed & Ka'Ryzma, who are my biggest cheerleaders. Thank you for showing me unconditional love and supporting me in everything that I do. You three are the greatest gifts that God has given me and I love each of you very much.

To Lynetta Jordan, for mentoring me and showing me the ropes of publishing my first book. You have inspired me over the years. Thank you for all you've done. Love you to life.

AND TO MY HEAVENLY FATHER, WHO IS THE AUTHOR AND FINISHER OF MY FAITH. I GIVE HIM ALL THE GLORY, THE HONOR, AND THE PRAISE. I THANK HIM FOR LEADING ME THROUGH THE MOST DIFFICULT MOMENTS OF MY LIFE.

INTRODUCTION

For as long as Kassidy could remember, she knew that her life had a purpose. As a little girl, Kassie would dream big and it felt like she could have the whole world. When Kassie was young, she didn't know what "vision" meant but as she grew older she believe that God had given her a dream as a child concerning her life. She used to dream of being a famous singer and that her name would be known all over the world. Music was all around Kassidy from her mother's side to her father's side of the family.

Kassie's dad was named Henry, and he was a member of two Gospel groups, one consisted of his mother, sisters and brothers, and the other group was a male group. Boy did Henry love to sing, and could sing too. Henry had even cut a few albums with his family group and they are being played locally and in the surrounding areas. Kassie's mom was named Deborah, and she was a member of a local gospel group with her brother, Sam. Kassie's Uncle Sam, had been a musician since he was a child. Kassie always considered them to be local "celebrities." Her uncle's gospel group would travel to sing from place to place and sometimes he would even give Kassie a solo to sing. Sam nurtured Kassie's gift and taught Kassie how to use her voice and to not be afraid to sing publicly.

Growing up it appeared as if Kassidy's family had it all together.

Kassidy's grandma was named Florida and she was a devoted Christian who loved the Lord and always kept the family together, she was the glue. Every time the doors of the church were open, there was a guarantee that Kassie's grandma Florida was in there. She made sure that everyone went to church every Sunday, even when they didn't want to. Kassie looked up to her grandmother because she demonstrated so much strength and she wanted to be just like her. Kassie would often call her grandma when she needed prayer concerning any situation. Kassie knew that if her grandmother prayed for her, that everything was going to be alright. Kassie knew that God listened to her grandmother because she was so faithful.

Kassie's grandfather was named Oliver and he was the provider of the family, he was the rock. He was a quiet man who didn't have much education. As a matter of fact once Kassie's mother told her that her grandfather couldn't read, Kassie would read to him often and try to teach him what she knew. He would just smile and say "Kassie, its ok." Kassie's grandfather was biracial. His mother was African American and his father was Caucasian. Kassie always admired her grandfather and always enjoyed her time with him. He was the first and only man in Kassie's life that ever made her feel like she was important and really showed her unconditional love. Oliver was Kassie's heart and she was his.

Henry's mother and father was devoted Christians as well. Henry's mother was a Deaconess and his father was the Associate Pastor of their family church.   However, Kassidy didn't get to see her paternal grandparents as much in the earlier part of her life.

When Kassie's mom and dad first married they lived with her maternal grandparents, and uncle Sam.   After two years of marriage Kassidy's parents had her older sister Kennedy.   Two years later, Kassidy was born and they all lived in one big house for the next five years. Kassidy's mother, Deborah only has two daughters which were Kennedy and Kassidy, but that wasn't the same for her father Henry. Henry had five daughters in total.

Henry conceived two daughters from his first marriage the oldest was Bianca, and the second oldest was Lori.   Henry conceived two daughters from his second marriage which were Kennedy and Kassidy. Henry also had another daughter named Quanah, in which you will read about in this story. Later Henry married his third wife, which becomes Kassidy's stepmom. Now that you have the foundation of where it all began, allow me to tell you Kassidy's story.

CHAPTER 1:

AS A CHILD

Kassidy was born April 10th, 1983, in a small town in North Carolina known as Tyner. As a young girl she saw the world as a safe and happy place. A place where she would grow up to become what she wanted to be in life. Kassie was so sure how her life would turn out and she knew that she would finish high school, go to college, have a great career, get married, have children and live a great life. But things don't always turn out the way we plan them.

Church was a big part of Kassie's family lives. They would go to church sometimes two or three times a week. Kassidy and Kennedy were members of a few choirs the mass choir and junior choir. They were also members of the junior usher board at their church. Kassie loved to sing and wasn't shy to sing in front a crowd. A seed was planted in Kassie's life at an early age that would stick with her over the years.

When Kassie was 5 years old, she, her dad, mom, and sister moved to their own home down the street from her grandparent's house. When they first moved in, life was great. Henry worked at a shipyard in Newport News, Virginia and he was an officer of the National Guard. He had retired from the Army reserves previously. Deborah helped her brother by running errands for him at his beauty salon and being his assistant. Kassie's mother was spoiled rotten. Indeed she was an adult, but she would pout like a child and would stop at nothing to get what she wanted. Not only was Henry financially supporting Deborah, but she was getting financial support from her father Oliver and her brother Sam. Deborah utilized the money that she got from Henry to help take care of the bills and necessities, and her father and brother would give her allowance to shop and buy whatever she wanted or thought she needed.

Over the next few years, life started to take a toll on Kassie's mom and dad's relationship. Henry had become distant and didn't spend much time with his family anymore. Henry was all about work, his singing groups and the National Guard, and Deborah didn't help the situation any better because she was all about going shopping on a regular basis, buying the latest labels, eating out and looking good. So they grew apart.

As time continued to pass, Kassie's parents would argue over the smallest things and for Kassie home didn't feel like home anymore. Deborah became very jealous over Henry and would react in public by making scenes, especially if she saw Henry talking to other women.

Henry lost his father in January of 1994 which only added more stress upon their marriage. Henry and Deborah's love for each other was fading and Henry started to see another woman. Once Deborah discovered that Henry was dating another woman, she was hurt and became enraged, especially when she found out who the woman was. The woman's name was Racheal. Deborah considered Racheal to be a friend of hers. Deborah would visit the Racheal often and give her rides, advice and sometimes even money when she was having a hard time financially. So of course, this was very difficult for Deborah to deal with.

Henry and Deborah's marriage had finally ran its course and Henry decided to move out. When Henry left, it seemed as if he took Deborah's soul with him. Before he left Deborah was a very outgoing person who spoke her mind with confidence and didn't care what people thought about her. But once they separated, Deborah became very depressed and would sleep for days at a time. She wouldn't leave the house and didn't want much company in the home. This went on for at least six months to a year after Henry left.

A year past and Deborah finally started to come around, but she would never be the same. She became this bitter and mean person, and she took all of her anger out on Kassidy and Kennedy. Deborah would say that they reminded her of Henry and would beat them most of the time for no apparent reason. Deborah thought that if she hurt Kennedy and Kassidy, that she was hurting Henry. This was Deborah's revenge towards Henry, but it didn't work.

The same year that Henry moved out, Kassie's grandfather Oliver died from a stroke a few days before Christmas of 1994. "The rock" of the family was gone and it affected everyone that was connected to him. Deborah felt like she had lost two of the most important men in her life, her husband and her father.

When things got rough and they often did, Kassie would call her grandmother Florida for prayer. Her grandmother would always pray for Kassie but after a while her grandmother started to encourage Kassie to pray for herself and her family. Grandma Florida told Kassidy, "You are chosen by God and if you pray to God yourself, he would listen to you also. Trust him and never doubt him." Grandma Florida also told Kassie, "God has no respect of persons." Kassie didn't understand so she asked her grandmother, "What does that mean?" Grandma Florida responded softly, "It means God does not show favoritism sweetie, he will listen to you just as he listens to me. Just because you are young, it doesn't mean that he doesn't hear you if you pray."

Kassie always listened to her grandmother because she knew that Grandma Florida held much wisdom and whatever she spoke out of her mouth was as good as gold. Kassie was amazed at her grandmother's strength and how she could always talk to people in a calm manner, never raising her voice. Grandmother Florida had the power to talk sense into anybody who was upset or had lost their way.

Kassie's sister Lori was getting married and she wanted Kennedy and Kassidy to be junior bridesmaids in her wedding. One day, Lori met with Deborah, Kennedy and Kassidy in a store. Lori asked Deborah if she could take Kennedy and Kassidy with her to get fitted for shoes for the wedding. Deborah agreed and said that it was ok. So Lori took off with the girls to the shoe store.

While at the store, Lori was talking to Kennedy and Kassidy and asked, "How have things been since dad moved out?" Kassidy and Kennedy told Lori everything that had been happening since their father left. They couldn't keep it a secret any longer. They told Lori how Deborah was beating them every time she was angry or frustrated with Henry. Lori thought it was unfair for her sisters to be treated that way so she contacted their oldest sister, Bianca and informed her.

The next day Lori and Bianca called their dad, Henry and informed him of how Deborah had been mistreating the girls. The next day Kennedy and Kassidy went to live with their father. It was a big difference for Kennedy and Kassidy because they were used to being around their friends and family, but they knew at that time that they couldn't continue to stay in the situation that we were in. Kassidy and Kennedy stayed with our dad for a few weeks but that didn't last very long because Rachael, their dad's girlfriend was used to having Henry's attention to herself and this caused problems between them. Rachael wanted the girls to go, so Henry decided that they should leave. He made arrangements for Kassidy and Kennedy to stay with his sister, their aunt.

Henry asked his youngest sister, Tracy if Kassidy and Kennedy could stay with her family for a while. Tracy agreed and the girls stayed with her for a couple of weeks but Tracy had her own children to care for and it wasn't fair that Henry wasn't helping out financially. So Henry asked his niece, Tonya if Kassidy and Kennedy could stay with her and her daughter. Tonya agreed that the girls could stay, but that didn't last very long either. Tonya was very controlling and meticulous about everything. So a few weeks later, Kassidy and Kennedy begged their father to let them stay with his oldest sister instead, which was Tonya's mother.

Kassidy and Kennedy thought it would be a great idea to stay with their aunt Betty, because she always make them feel welcome when they would go visit her. Betty had two of her grandchildren living with her that were around Kassidy and Kennedy's age. In their aunt Betty's house lived her husband Nathan, her daughter, Kelly, Kelly's son Sterling and Betty's granddaughter Amy.

For the first couple of weeks, the family made Kennedy and Kassidy feel welcomed, safe and loved, but after a while everything changed. I guess their family grew tired of Kassidy and Kennedy and felt like we were in the way. The family knew Kassidy and Kennedy's story and that they had been through a lot with their mom and dad. But that didn't stop Kelly and her sister Tasha from harassing and making hurtful comments towards Kassidy and Kennedy. Tasha and Kelly would say

10

things such as, "Your mom nor dad doesn't want you, that's why you are living here with our parents."

Kassidy and Kennedy were treated differently from the other children in the home. Kassidy and Kennedy were accused of stealing their hygiene products and clothes. Nathan would periodically check Kassidy and Kennedy's bags to see if they had taken Amy's clothes or belongings, only to find that nothing was stolen. This affected how Kassidy and Kennedy once felt about their family. They knew that something had to change and change fast.

So Kassidy and Kennedy started building a new relationship with their mom by talking with her on the phone from time to time. Deborah even started visiting Kassidy and Kennedy, and they realized that she had indeed changed from being a mean person. After a while Kennedy and Kassidy realized that the family that they thought they wanted to get to know and live with so badly, wasn't who they thought they were. So they decided the best thing for them to do was move back home with their mom and they did.

CHAPTER 2

THERE'S NO PLACE LIKE HOME

When Kassidy and Kennedy moved back with their mom, things were really different. Deborah wasn't that "mean" person that she was before the girls left. Deborah had become very meek and humble and didn't say much. Deborah was just so glad to have her girls back and she was afraid to lose them again. Deborah knew she needed to change her behavior towards the girls, which was a great thing. Kassidy and Kennedy reconnected with their family and friends from their hometown.

Kassidy and Kennedy had to get use to the financial change that had taken place since their dad left and grandfather died. Reality had set in and they realized that their financial circumstance had decreased from what they once were accustomed to. The support from their grandfather Oliver and dad Henry were gone, and that took some time for them to adjust.

Although Henry was paying child support for Kassidy and Kennedy, it still was a struggle for them. Kassidy and Kennedy had become accustomed to a lavish lifestyle shopping at all the high-end stores such as SEARS, MACY'S, BELK'S and JC PENNY'S. They didn't know what it was like to shop at Super 10, Roses or the bargain stores but they were about to find out.

13

Kassie's mom had to apply for welfare because she was not generating enough money to provide for her family on her own. Kassie and Kennedy were embarrassed because of what they heard the children at school say about welfare. When they would go grocery shopping with their mom and she would pull out her paper food stamps to pay for the food, and they would ask to go to the car. This was in the mid-90s, which was before the EBT cards was used instead of paper food stamps. Eventually, they got over the embarrassment, once they realized that there were many other families that were on welfare.

Kassidy and Kennedy realized that things would never be the same again and the life that they once knew was over. Deborah sat down with her daughters one day and had a heart to heart conversation about their future. Deborah told her daughters, "Look at my life. I quit my job and allowed your father to take care of me. Now I am alone with no means of income for myself and my whole lifestyle has changed in a blink of an eye. Never depend on a man or anybody else to take care of you. Stay in school and further your education, do better than I did." Those words of encouragement never left Kassidy's mind because she saw what her mother went through when her father left and she was determined not to repeat that cycle. Kassie wanted so much more for her life and had big dreams of getting them.

Since Deborah wasn't as strict anymore, Kassidy and Kennedy felt like they could do whatever they wanted. Deborah gave the girls a lot of space because she was afraid that they would leave her again, and Kassidy and Kennedy took advantage of that. The girls would have friends come over to the house and sometimes they would spend the night. Needless to say those friends were boys, and Deborah didn't mind them staying over because she wanted to please her daughters.

Their friends would hang out and watch television, listen to music, smoke marijuana, drink alcohol, and of course make out. Deborah sometimes would even purchase the alcohol for her daughters because she said if they were going to drink or smoke, she would rather they did it in front of her. She knew she couldn't stop them from drinking but she at least wanted to be able to monitor their intake and behavior.

The summer after Kassidy's 7th grade year, she lost her virginity. Kassie was only 13 years old. At the time she thought she was ready and mature enough to handle that type of decision, but she wasn't. Kassie was looking for love in all the wrong places because she was missing her dad's presence and attention.

Later that year, Kassie joined the basketball team at her school. She enjoyed going to the away games it was a great experience for her. It was exciting for her to be on the team because she loved to play basketball and could play. Deborah and Kennedy supported Kassie at every game, but Henry never attended any of the games because he was always too busy doing something else.

The summer before 9th grade, Kassie joined the high school cheerleading team. It was something new and challenging for Kassie to do. Kassie always found the thrill in trying something new and different. She would get bored with routine so she would always be looking for something different to get into. Kassie was on the junior varsity cheerleading squad and Kennedy was on the varsity squad. After the first few weeks, Kassie began to get used to the practices and hard workouts and started to even enjoy it.

A few weeks before school started Kassie's sister, Kennedy found out that she was pregnant so she couldn't cheer on the varsity squad anymore; she was only 16 years old.

On the first day of school, Kassidy participated in the school's Pep Rally. That was the moment when everyone in the school found out who was on the football team and the cheerleading squad for that school year. Kassie had to perform in the gym in front of the entire school, and she was very nervous. After it was over, Kassie was so relieved and ecstatic. She felt great about her first performance as a cheerleader in front of the entire school.

Kassidy and Kennedy were two years apart and very close as sisters. Kassidy always looked up to Kennedy. For many years they dressed alike, from Kassidy's birth until Kassidy was in the 10th grade in high school. Kennedy was a basketball player in middle so Kassidy became a player when she was in middle school. Kennedy was a cheerleader her freshman and sophomore year of high school, so Kassidy became a cheerleader her freshman year of high school. Kassidy enjoyed her freshman year of high school, especially during homecoming season.

It was time to nominate students to be homecoming representative for each class. The morning of nominations, Kassidy's homeroom teacher asked the class who they wanted to nominate for homecoming queen for the freshman class. Everyone started raising their hands and calling out names to the teacher. Then one of Kassie's classmates called her name as a possible nominee and the teacher, put Kassie's name on the board.

Kassie's teacher's name was Mr. Lewis. Kassie was embarrassed and didn't want to get disappointed if she didn't win, so she asked Mr. Lewis to take her name off of the board. Mr. Lewis erased Kassie's name, and then asked if he could speak to her outside of the classroom.

Once they walked outside of the room, Mr. Lewis asked, "Why don't you want your name written down as a nominee?" Kassie responded, "I didn't want to be disappointed if I didn't win." He said, "You never know if you don't try, let's just put your name on the list and see what happens." Kassie said, "Okay."

A few weeks later the votes were tallied and it was time to announce the winners for each grade. The secretary started with the freshman class and she announced, "The 1997 Homecoming representative for the freshman class is Kassidy Bell." Kassidy's mouth dropped, and she couldn't believe it. Her class cheered for her. At the end of the day Kassidy saw her teacher Mr. Lewis, and gave him a big hug and said, "Thank you for believing in me and encouraging me to go for it."

Kassidy had never been so excited in her life. She had to purchase two different gowns, one for the parade and one for the homecoming ceremony on the football field. Participating in the homecoming parade was a great feeling for Kassidy. She felt like a celebrity.

When Kassidy participated in the Homecoming ceremony, she asked her friend to escort her on the field. She wore a beautiful black and white gown with white gloves. When her name was called they put a banner on Kassie, gave her a bouquet of flowers and took her picture to put in the local newspaper. Kassidy was on cloud nine all night. Not only were the picture in the newspaper but it was in the school yearbook later that year. That experience planted a seed in Kassidy and she wanted that feeling again.

CHAPTER 3

FINDING INDEPENDENCE

Kassidy's tenth grade year, she decided not to continue her journey as a cheerleader and become more focused on her classwork and getting a job. Kassie was 15 years old when her mom signed for her to get a work permit so that she could work as well. Kassidy got her first job at McDonald's with her sister. It made Kassie feel great to make her own money, it gave her confidence and independence. All she wanted to do was to buy her own clothes and shoes. Kassidy worked at McDonalds for almost three months. Her time was cut short at McDonalds when she requested a Saturday off because she wanted to go to her cousin's funeral.

Kassie worked her regular shift the morning of the funeral. When it was time for Kassie to get off, her manager informed her that she had to stay on the clock because they were really busy. Kassie told her manager that she was previously approved for the day off and that she was leaving whether he liked it or not. The manager was angry with Kassie because she wouldn't bend and she stood her ground. So he told Kassie, "If you leave, don't bother coming back to work." Kassie looked at her manager, grabbed her belongings and walked out of the door. That was Kassidy's last day as an employee at McDonald's.

Working at McDonald's was a great experience for Kassie, but she needed a job with a little more freedom. So she decided to work for her Uncle Sam at his beauty salon. Kassie only worked at the salon after school and on the weekends. Kassie's Uncle Sam taught her everything he knew about styling hair. She started off as an assistant by shampooing and conditioning the clients hair, but after a while she was completing the entire hair style for his clients as well. Sam would pay Kassidy at the end of each day for helping him. She was able to buy her own school clothes, shoes, and her hair stayed "fly" most of the time.

Kassie's sister, Kennedy gave birth to a baby girl and named her Khloe. Although Kennedy gave birth to Khloe, it was as if Kassidy had gained a child. Kennedy remained active in sports after she had her daughter and continued to work at McDonald's so Kassidy helped out with her niece, Khloe. Every morning Kassie took Khloe's bath and dressed her for the day. For birthdays and holiday's Kassie would buy Khloe clothes and gifts with the money that she made. Kassie loved Khloe like she was her own. Most of Kassie's time spent would be with Khloe, when she wasn't in school or working. Sometimes Khloe would even be with Kassidy at the salon while she was working.

Deborah felt like she fell as a mother because Kennedy had a baby at an early age. In a small town where they lived, the people in the community and church made Deborah feel that way because it was frowned upon to have a baby out of wedlock and especially at a young age. But today, this is a very common thing.

One day Kennedy informed her mom that Kassidy was no longer a virgin. Kennedy said she got tired of her mom thinking that Kassidy was the "angel" child and putting her on a petal stool. Deborah was upset with Kassidy and didn't speak to her for a few days, but after a while she came around. Kassidy didn't get angry with Kennedy for telling her mom. As a matter of fact, Kassidy was kind of relieved. Kassie didn't have to lie or hide her secret anymore. Kassie was an Aries, and it was very difficult for her to lie. If you know anything about an Aries, you know that they are not good liars because they are so direct and straightforward. Kassidy wanted to tell her mother for a long time but she didn't know how.

During Kassie's junior year in high school, she started thinking about what she wanted to do after she graduated from high school. So Kassie started buckling down in her studies and she made "A & B" honor roll and sometimes "A" honor roll. Kassie still wasn't sure about what her future goals were but she knew that she wanted to further her education.

After school, Kassie continued to go to the salon to help her uncle. Sometimes Kassie would hang outside of the salon, and she was exposed to the street life. The salon was located in a very busy part of Edenton, NC. So Kassie would hang outside with her friends or walk the streets to the hang out spots. On the weekends, Kassie went to the local clubs or lounges with Kennedy and her friends. Kassie stayed out all night, until the next morning most of the time.

Kassidy was only 16 years old at the time and she was going to clubs every weekend, drinking, smoking and doing whatever she wanted to do. In the late 90s, club owners weren't checking for identification cards. So there wasn't really an age limit of who was allowed in the club. Kassidy would hang out with Kennedy and her friends who were older than Kassie. Kassie had friends her age too but she liked hanging out with the older girls at times.

Kassie's junior year of high school, she started dating a guy name Kent. Kent had graduated a few years earlier from high school. When Kassidy was a freshman, Kent was a senior. This relationship started when Kassidy approached him and asked him if he would accompany her to her junior prom. Kassidy was always mature for her age, which is why she never was interested in guys her age. They exchanged phone numbers and Kent said he would be honored to take Kassie to the prom. When Kent called Kassie he told her that he had a secret crush on her for years when we were in school together.

Kassidy really liked Kent very much and he wasn't the "pretty boy" type, he was more of a "bad guy." For a guy to get Kassie's attention, he had to have a certain type of charisma about him. In this case, Kent very was street smart and intelligent. The fact that Kent completed high school was a plus and Kassie admired that about him. Kassidy loved to make others laugh and she loved if someone could make her laugh as well, and Kent did that. They had so much fun when they were together. Kent had the gift to make people notice him and Kassie definitely noticed.

The first time Kassidy really took notice of Kent was on a Friday night and Kassie and her friends were hanging out on the block. The block was packed with guys and girls. There were people standing on each side of the street and Kent was amongst the crowd. A few of the guys started rapping in the middle of the street and battling each other. Kent was the last one to rap because he allowed everyone to go before him. But when it was Kent's turn to battle, he destroyed the competition. Kent's lyrics were so powerful and entertaining at the same time. People could never get angry with him because he was so comical. Kent and his crew even formed a local rap group called The Crime Mob.

For the first three months of their relationship, Kassidy and Kent dated and spent a lot of time together. Kassidy really like Kent and knew that he was someone special so they decided to take their time getting to know each other. They became best friends and were very close. For holidays, Kent would bring gifts to school for Kassie which made her feel very special. Kent would walk to the high school every morning to spend time with her before the morning bell rung. He would even come to the school in the rain, which showed Kassie how dedicated he was to her.

Kent would page Kassie daily saying "I love you" or "thinking of you."

When Kassie and Kent weren't together, they were on the phone talking to each other for hours. Of course in every relationship there is always something or someone that will cause drama. Kent had an ex-girlfriend who was older than him and she was CRAZY!!! Although they were no longer in a relationship, Kent's ex-girlfriend refused to let go. She would call Kassie and harass her on the phone. She even stalked Kassie and Kent by following them around town. One time Kent's ex-girlfriend came to the high school to proposition Kassie to fight her after school. She threatened Kassie constantly, but Kassie wasn't intimidated by her and continued her relationship with Kent. Kassidy wasn't going to allow anyone to interfere with her relationship with Kent..

A week before prom, Kent told Kassie that he wouldn't be able to take her to the prom. Kassie asked Kent, "Why?" Kent informed Kassie that his ex-girlfriend threatened to harm her if he went to the prom with her. Kent told Kassidy that he was protecting her by not going with her to the prom. Kassidy didn't like it but she respected his decision not to go. Kassie decided to go to the prom alone.

However, Kassie's cousin called her and told her that one of her classmates didn't have a date and that he had already purchased his tuxedo. Kassie received a phone call from her classmate and they coordinated their colors which wasn't very hard to do since Kassie gown was silver and his tuxedo was white.

Kassie went to the prom with her classmate and they had a wonderful evening. They danced, took pictures, and ate. Just when the prom was almost over Kassie went over to her classmate and thanked him for a wonderful evening. Kassie soon left the prom with her friends and they picked Kent up so that they could spend the rest of the evening together. A group of Kassie's friends spent the night at a motel and Kent was with her. They enjoyed the evening together and went their separate ways the next morning.

CHAPTER 4

SHATTERED

It was the end Kassie's junior year and she was excited to become a senior in high school the following school year. Kassidy was still working at her uncle's beauty salon and still clubbing every weekend during the summer. Kent and Kassidy's relationship was still going strong and they spent as much time together as they possibly could.

There was another local rap group in Edenton called, The Original Gangsters and they were rivals to The Crime Mob. Instead of coming together and making music, they begin to despise each other. A local club owner decided to have rap wars on the weekends which caused great tension between the two groups.

Kent was the leader of The Crime Mob group and a guy named King was the leader of The Original Gangsters. Kassie and King had actually become friends with each other and were planning to collaborate on a song together. King wanted Kassidy and Kennedy to sing the hook (chorus) of a song that he had been working on. They had even rehearsed the song a few times already, but didn't get a chance to make it in the studio. Nobody knew about the collaboration, not even Kent. Kassidy knew that if Kent found out about the collaboration, that he would become upset. So Kassidy kept it to herself.

One night in a local club, there was a rap battle and a fight occurred between the two groups. Each group begin plotting on what they were going to do to the other. Kassidy and Kent didn't go to the club that night, because they had decided to spend time together instead. The next morning they both received calls that a fight had occurred at the club the night before and it was causing so much turmoil. Then Kent received a phone call from one of his friends, and he pressured Kent to go with him to retaliate on the group.

Kassidy begged Kent not to leave her to go with his friend. Kassie knew in her heart that if Kent left that something horrible was going to happen, she could feel it. Kassidy always had a strong intuition that would let her know when something bad was about to happen. Kent allowed himself to be persuaded by his friend and left Kassidy's side anyway.

Kassie cried, because deep down inside she knew that it would be the last time that she would see Kent for a while. So Kassie walked to her friend's house which was a few houses away, where her sister Kennedy was. Kennedy had spent the night at this friend's house and she was there waiting for Kassidy to arrive so that she could take her home.

When Kassie and Kennedy arrived home, they were still tired from the night before so they each took a nap. When they woke up, Deborah asked them to go to the grocery store because she needed a few items.

Right before they were about to leave for the store, the phone ranged. It was one of their friends calling to inform them that the two rap groups were planning to meet later that day to "squash the beef." Kassie became worried and asked her friend to keep her posted on what was going on.

Kassidy and Kennedy left and went to the grocery store to get items for their mom. They called their mom to see if there was anything else that she needed before they left the store. Deborah informed the girls that she received another phone call from their friends. She told her daughters that King from Original Gangsters had been shot and the shooter was a guy from The Crime Mob. The news bothered Kassidy and Kennedy and they began to pray for King hoping that he would be okay.

Once they arrived back home, Kennedy ran to the house first with some of the groceries, while Kassidy gathered the rest of the items from the car. Kassidy entered her house and immediately her antenna went up. The dead silence in the house was so loud, it was hard for Kassie not to notice. She looked at her mom and sister and noticed the tears streaming down their faces.

Kassie's heart began to race because she knew that it wasn't good news that she was about to hear. Kassie finally asked, "Ma, what's wrong?" Deborah replied, "I received another call from a friend of yours. She said that King is dead and Kent is the one who shot him. Now Kent is on the run hiding from the police." Kassie's heart skipped a beat and it felt like her heart was ripped out of her chest and immediately she fell to the ground. She couldn't fathom the thought that her friend King was dead, and her boyfriend Kent was the shooter. She had lost two people who she knew and had grown to care about. Kassidy's heart was broken!!!

Kennedy wanted to ride to town to check on their friends and inquire about what really happened. Kennedy asked Kassidy to go with her but Kassie was hesitant at first. Kassie didn't think it was a good idea because she knew that people were upset with Kent for shooting King. When Kassidy and Kennedy arrived to their friend's house, their friends took their frustrations out on Kassidy. They tormented Kassidy with their hurtful words, slandering Kent every chance they got. They asked Kassidy, "How can you still love him after he murdered someone?" They never once thought about how Kassie was feeling on the inside and how broken she was behind all of this.

Kassidy walked away and began to cry because she wasn't given a chance to express how she was feeling about the incident. Kassidy couldn't understand how they could be so angry at her when she wasn't the one that pulled the trigger. They didn't understand or realize Kassie's pain and the fact that she was really affected by the situation because she had lost two people that she truly cared about.

Kassie told her sister that she didn't want to be around them for a while after that. Kassie couldn't stand to hear negative things that were being said about Kent. Kassie knew that Kent wasn't a bad person and that he just got caught up in a bad situation. Being at the wrong place at the wrong time.

This was very hard for Kassie to deal with. It seemed like her life had flipped upside down. For the next few days, everywhere that Kassie went people were talking about Kent and what happened to King. Kent's picture was even in the newspaper and on the news. People in the community would stop and stare at Kassie because most of them knew that Kent was her boyfriend.

So for the following three weeks Kassie stayed home and didn't leave to go anywhere. She had gone into a deep stage of depression. Kassie had not heard from Kent because he was still on the run from the police. Kassie was informed that Kent's life was in danger if King's crew or family found him before the police did. Kassie was also told that King's family had threatened her life if Kent didn't turn himself in to the police.

Kent wouldn't write or call Kassidy because he was afraid that the letters or phone calls would lead the police to him. This was very frustrating for Kassidy because she had become so accustomed to talking to Kent every day. Kassidy slept most of the time. She wouldn't eat, or take a bath at times. She was losing her strength and will to live. The pressure of everything was becoming unbearable for Kassidy. Nobody could understand what she was going through on the inside and she felt so alone.

Kassidy would sit and cry, looking out of her window wondering where Kent was and if he was okay. It was at that very moment that Kassidy realized that a person's life could change just in an instant, because she knew that incident would change her life forever.

Kassidy missed Kent dearly, because he had become Kassidy's best friend, and she could talk to him about anything. They had spent so much time together and she never imagined her life without him. Kent had been on the run for almost a month and Kassie still hadn't heard from him.

Then one day Kassie received a phone call from someone who was obviously trying to disguise their voice as a female, but once Kassidy heard the voice she knew it was Kent. Kent tried to disguise his voice because he was certain that the police had the phone's tapped, and he didn't want to take any chances. All kinds of emotions came upon Kassie all at once as she began to sob while holding the phone to her ear. She asked Kent, "How are you and where are you?" But Kassie knew Kent couldn't tell her where he was, however he let her know that he was okay. Kassie told him that she loved him, that she was praying for him, and hoped to see him soon.

Soon after that phone call, the local detective's and sheriff's from the police department raided Kassie's home looking for Kent or clues to where he was located. Kassidy couldn't give them any information because she really didn't know where Kent was. Kassidy's home was raided again by the police within a few weeks later. The police encouraged Kassidy to contact them if she heard anything from Kent. The police claimed that they received an anonymous tip that Kent was hiding at Kassidy's home.

Each time Kassie's home was raided it was at least 15 officers in the home. The officers had rifles and sawed off shot guns, Kassie had never experienced anything like that before in her life. Kassie felt like she was living in a bad dream and couldn't wake up. On both occasions that the authorities came to Kassie's home, King's brothers and uncle came with them.

Once King's brothers learned where Kassidy lived, they would park across the street from her house all night, blasting their music and watching Kassie's home. Kassie didn't know whether they were watching to see if Kent would come outside or trying to intimidate Kassidy and her family. It infuriated Kassidy because she knew that Kent wasn't there but they wouldn't leave her alone. Kassie knew that King's family had the police in their pocket so she knew that she couldn't call on the authorities.

Kent had been on the run for over a month now, and Kassie's depression was getting worse. Her eyes were swollen from crying all day. She wouldn't talk to anyone because she didn't think anyone would understand what she was going through. Deborah became very worried about Kassidy so she contacted Kennedy who had moved to Raleigh, NC with Khloe's father. Deborah informed Kennedy how Kassidy was doing and encouraged her to talk to her sister. Kennedy drove from Raleigh to take Kassidy back to Raleigh with her for a few days. Kassidy agreed that she needed to get away from everything for a while to clear her head. So she packed some of her things and left with Kennedy.

They drove to Raleigh and stayed with some of Kennedy's friends. Everyone tried their best to cheer Kassidy up, but she continued to stay in a rut. Kennedy's friends were having a party and invited them to go. They arrived to the party and it was packed with guests, but Kassidy still wasn't feeling it. Kassidy began to drink at the party, which only made her feel worse. Kassie drank a few beers and all she could do was think about Kent.

Kassie questioned God and kept asking, "Why, did this have to happen to us?" The weekend was finally ending and Kennedy and her boyfriend decided to take Kassidy back home. On the way home, Kassie stared out the back window, looking at the sky. Suddenly, Kassie remembered what her grandmother told her about God hearing her prayers, so she began to pray. Kassie talked to God and asked him to give her peace. She also asked God to show her a sign that everything would be alright because she couldn't bare the pain anymore.

After Kassie finished her prayer, she looked up at the sky and she noticed one of the clouds was formed into the shape of something. She closed her eyes and opened them again only to look up at the sky and find that the shape of the cloud was still there. The cloud was the shape of a person's head and she could see a formation of ears on the sides of the head.

This freaked Kassidy out because she had never seen anything like that before. Kassie turned away from the image in the clouds and blinked a few times. She thought to herself, "Maybe I'm tripping!" She kept this to herself and didn't say anything to Kennedy about what she saw in the cloud. Kassie thought that it would make her sound crazy and as if she was losing her mind. Kassidy turned back to the window and looked at the cloud, and again the image was still there.

Kassie asked God, "What does this mean?" Kassie continued "God, what are you trying to tell me?" She then remembered her prayer to God and thought that maybe he had given her that sign. Only she didn't know exactly what the sign meant. Looking at the image in the cloud, Kassidy automatically assumed that it was Kent. But it confused her because she thought, "How could this be Kent? The image is a round bald looking head and Kent wore braids." The image wasn't making any sense to Kassie, so she just brushed it off.

CHAPTER 5

THE MISSING PIECE

Once Kassidy arrived home, she greeted her mother. Deborah informed Kassie that she had received several phone calls that day from Kent's brother, Junior and that he wanted Kassie to return his calls as soon as possible. Kassie called Junior back and someone answered and said, "Hello." Kassie asked, "Can I speak to Junior?" The person on the phone replied, "This is Junior." Immediately Kassie's stomach became upset, and her intuition started kicking into overdrive.

She knew that something strange was going on and that the person one the phone was not Junior. As Kassie continued to talk to this person, she recognized the voice and immediately knew exactly who she was talking to. It felt as if Kassie's heart dropped to the pit of her stomach and this made Kassie very anxious.

The person on the phone asked if she could come to Junior's house and Kassie agreed. The voice on the phone continued to insist that he was Junior, but Kassie knew better. Kassie asked Kennedy, "Can you take me to Junior's house?" Kassie pleaded with Kennedy and said, "It sounds important Kennedy, please take me." Kassidy continued, "But I have weird feeling that the person that I was talking to was not Junior."

This peaked Kennedy's curiosity and she agreed to take Kassie.

Once they arrived to Junior's house, Kassidy walked in the front door and the door closed behind her. Junior's mother said, "Hurry up and go out the back door. He's back there waiting for you. You need to get him out of here. I can't be harboring a fugitive." Kassie apparently confused at what she had just heard, responded, "Huh?"

Kassie went out of the back door and began walking down the stairs. As she walked towards the bottom of the stairs, Kassie noticed a figure standing underneath them. Kassidy asked, "Who is that?" The person walked from underneath the steps and Kassie didn't recognize who it was at first because they had a bald head. When Kassie got to the bottom of the stairs the person walked towards her. As the person got closer to Kassie, she realized it was Kent.

Everything started flashing in Kassie's mind. The bald headed image in the cloud that Kassie saw on her way back from Raleigh, was an image of Kent. That was the "sign" from God that Kassie prayed for in the car and God heard her prayer and answered it. It was God's way of telling Kassie that she would see him real soon. Then Kassie realized that her intuition wasn't lying to her when she knew that it wasn't Junior that she was talking to on the phone. She knew that it was Kent.

Kassidy grabbed Kent and they hugged each other so tight. Kassie didn't want to let Kent go. Kent held her as she lied on his chest. They got in Kennedy's car and drove to a remote area so they could talk and catch up.

Once they were alone, Kassidy asked Kent to tell her what really happened with him and King that day of the shooting. Kassidy needed to know what and how it happened because she couldn't see herself standing behind someone who intentionally murdered another human being.

Kent told Kassie that his crew were planning to "squash the beef" and they were going to meet King and his crew from The Original Gangsters. He said that one of his friend's gave him a gun and told him to hold it just in case if things went wrong. Kent stated that when they arrived to King's house, King was sitting on the porch playing a song. Once King saw them approaching he walked to the middle of the street to meet them. Kent said his friend did most of the talking to King and he was supposed to make peace with him, but the situation got out of hand.

One of the guys from The Original Gangsters displayed his gun. Therefore Kent displayed the gun that he was holding. Kent said, "Once King noticed the gun he ran towards me and we tussled over the gun. Then the gun fired off and the bullet hit King in the chest. That's when I turned and ran for my life." When Kent told Kassie the story, she believed him. She didn't want to believe that the man she loved would do something like that intentionally. After they spent a few hours together, they decided to take Kent to his cousin's house.

The next morning Kassie received a phone call that the police arrested Kent at his cousin's house earlier that morning. Kent called Kassie to let her know that he had been arrested and was safe. Kassie was actually relieved because she was tired of worrying where Kent was and if he was in a safe place. Kent was taken into custody at the Chowan County District Jail on June 18, 2000. Kassie and Kent wrote each other almost every week and they talked on the phone to each other every day, sometimes three times a day. Kassie visited Kent every Wednesday and Sunday faithfully. She was determined to stand by Kent's side through all of it. Kassie went to some of Kent's court dates. Kent's friends, family and Kassie would put money in his canteen often. Kent had obtained so much money that he had reached his limit.

One day during a visit Kassie had with Kent, he asked Kassie to marry him. Of course, she said "Yes." So Kent signed over his canteen money to be released to Kassie so she could pick out and purchase their wedding rings set. Kent's brother went with Kassie when she purchased the ring. There were only a few of Kassie's family and friends that supported her decision to marry Kent. The rest of her family thought that Kassie was "Crazy."

Later that same day Kassidy and Kennedy went to visit their dad, Henry. Kassidy told her dad that she was getting married. Henry responded, "Have you lost your mind?" Kassie thought that her dad would understand and respect her decision, but he didn't. Kassie felt like her father was being a hypocrite, because she was hoping that he would understand her position especially when no one wanted him to marry his new wife. Kassie was hoping that he would have been more empathetic to what she was feeling and wanted. But Henry wouldn't budge regarding his opinion about Kassie marrying Kent. Henry just wanted the best for his baby girl, but Kassie didn't see it that way.

While they were visiting their dad, their step mother, Rachael asked the girls if she could talk to them in her bedroom. Once they were in the bedroom, Rachael said, "I am very angry with you two." Kassidy and Kennedy looked at each other confused and asked, "For what reason?" Rachael replied, "Why didn't you tell me that you had another sister?" Kassidy and Kennedy looked at each other again and asked, "What are you talking about?" Rachael continued, "A few nights ago, your dad told me that he conceived another daughter when he was separated from his first wife." Then she said, "It wasn't until after he married your mom when he found out that he had another child."

Kassidy and Kennedy were in shock and it was difficult for them to understand why their dad never told them. The girls approached Henry and asked him about what Rachael had told them. They wanted to hear his side of the story. After hearing what their father had to say, Kassidy and Kennedy asked , "What is her name?" "Where does she live and how can we get in touch with her?" Henry told Kassidy and Kennedy, "Her name is Quanah." Henry provided his daughters with Quanah's number and address. They soon left and headed to the address that their dad gave them. They wanted to meet Quanah and introduce themselves to her.

Kassidy and Kennedy arrived at Quanah's house and there was a guy on the porch holding a baby. The girls approached the guy and asked him if Quanah was home. The guy asked, "Who wants to know?" Kassie said, "My name is Kassidy and this is my sister, Kennedy. We believe that Quanah might be our sister and we want to meet her." His whole facial expression changed and he began to smile. He said, "Wow, Quanah told me that she had more sisters that I didn't know about, but I didn't believe her."

The guy told Kassidy and Kennedy that he was Quanah's boyfriend and that she wasn't home at the moment. He told them that she was working at Belk's in the mall. The girls asked, "Do you think it's a good idea to go to her job to meet her?" He said, "Yes, that would be fine." Kassidy and Kennedy left and headed to the mall.

Kassidy was excited and amazed at what kind of day it was becoming. Kassie had purchased her engagement ring and now was about to meet her sister for the very first time. When they arrived at the mall, Kassidy became nervous. She didn't know what type of person she was about to meet and didn't know if Quanah even wanted to meet them.

Kassidy and Kennedy didn't know what they were about to walk into.

Once they walked in the store, they noticed a woman at a station and the girls approached her and asked, "Excuse me, is Quanah working today?" The lady said while pointing, "Yes, she is working over there." Kassidy and Kennedy started walking towards the direction where the lady pointed. They noticed a women standing behind a register. A knot hit Kassidy's stomach as she turned to Kennedy and said, "Oh my God, I think that's her!" Kassidy continued, "She looks just like dad and Bianca."

Once they approached the lady, Kassie asked, "Is Quanah working today?" The girl turned and looked at Kassie with an attitude and responded, "I'm Quanah and who wants to know?" Kassie responded excitedly, "I'm Kassidy and this is Kennedy, and we believe that we are your sisters." Quanah's facial expression changed as she began to smile with her eyes filling up with tears and she hugged her sisters. Quanah said that she always knew that she had sisters but she was afraid to say anything to anybody. Quanah didn't think that anyone would believe her so she just kept it to herself.

Kassidy and Kennedy went home and called Bianca and Lori to inform them of everything that had transpired that day. They couldn't believe what they were hearing from Kassie and Kennedy and they were very confused. However, Bianca and Lori wanted to meet their sister. They couldn't understand why their dad, Henry kept it a secret from them for all those years. Henry didn't think about how his secret was affecting other people in his life, especially Quanah. Quanah had to keep her identity a secret for years to protect her father. Just imagine the stress that it put on Quanah all of those years.

The sisters planned a meet and greet for Bianca and Lori to meet Quanah. When Lori and Bianca finally met Quanah they talked for hours. They were getting to know one another, and Quanah fit right in with her sisters. Quanah had the most amazing spirit about her, and her smile made everyone feel comfortable around her. Quanah was the missing link that the sisters needed. They grew to love her just like she had always been a part of their lives.

CHAPTER 6

DECISIONS

Kassidy went to visit Kent at the jail and she told him everything that happened with her finding out about her sister and meeting her for the first time. Kassie always kept Kent in the loop of what was going on with her everyday life. She was always upfront with him and she expected the same in return.

When it was time for Kassie to go back to school, she was entering as a senior. She was only enrolled to go to school for the first semester, because she had completed all of the required courses for graduation. Since it was Kassie's senior year of high school, she really wanted to have a strong finish, so she became very focused on her school work and kept her grades up. Kassie wasn't able to visit Kent as much as before because she was so focused on her grades. The first visit that Kassie missed, Kent allowed some of friends to visit him instead.

On the following visit, Kassie went to see Kent. As she was signing her name she noticed Kent's ex-girlfriend's name on the list from the visit before. She had visited him on the day that Kassidy couldn't visit him. Kassie felt sick on her stomach and became very upset. Once Kent entered the visitation room, Kassie immediately asked him, "Why did you allow her to visit you?" Kent responded with a smirk on his face, "She wanted to see me."

Kassie was hurt and soon left that visit before her time was exhausted. Kent called Kassie several times at her uncle's salon where he knew that Kassie would be. When Kassie finally answered his call, she told Kent that she needed some space from him. Kassie needed to process the entire situation. She couldn't believe that Kent would allow his ex-girlfriend visit him after all that she had put them through. Kassie was sacrificing so much to be with Kent and she was starting to question herself if it was even worth it.

After the visit Kassidy started weaning herself away from Kent. She kept her communication with him limited and she didn't visit him as much as before. Kassidy began putting the energy that she had been given Kent, towards her family, friends and herself.

One night Kassie ran into an old friend of hers named Eric. They spent some time talking and catching up on lost time. Eric was several years older than Kassie but they were very good friends. Kassie could talk to him about anything and he would give her advice and a listening ear.

Kassie asked Eric if he could take her home. Eric asked Kassie, "So what's been going on in your life?" Kassie begin to tell Eric all that she was going through with Kent, school and her life. Eric listened to Kassie's concerns and allowed her to vent her frustrations. She told Eric about how upset she became when she discovered that Kent's ex-girlfriend visited him. Eric also told Kassie that he knew Kent's ex-girlfriend very well and that he had spoken with her recently. Eric told Kassie that Kent had been calling and writing his ex-girlfriend as well. Kassidy was very hurt by what Eric told her but she knew she needed to hear the truth.

The next time Kent called Kassie, she confronted him about the phone calls and letters to his ex-girlfriend. At first Kent tried to deny it, but Kassie was so persistent and adamant about knowing the truth. Kent finally admitted it and said, "Yes I've been writing her and calling her." Kassie then replied, "I have one more question for you. Before all the shooting happened, were you faithful to me the entire time?" Kent sighed and responded, "No, I wasn't." Kassie replied, "That's all I needed to know" and she hung up the phone. Kassie always had faith in Kent up until that very moment, and she was tired being lied to.

Kassidy cried not because her relationship was over, but because she was about to sacrifice her life and support Kent, when he wasn't being honest with her. Kassie had stopped talking to some of her friends and family because they didn't support her relationship with Kent. Kassie was loyal to Kent the entire time they were together. But once Kassie found out that Kent had not been faithful to her, she realized she couldn't do it anymore.

Kassie felt that only a "fool" would stand by a man who couldn't be faithful to her when he was a free man and now expecting her to be faithful to him while Kent serve his prison sentence. So Kassie stopped writing Kent letters. She stopped visiting him and receiving his phone calls. Kassie felt like all that she had allowed herself to go through was for nothing. Kassie felt like Kent had made a complete fool out of her and she was determined not to be his fool anymore. Kassie was determined to complete high school so she returned her focus back on her school work so that she could finish her last semester.

Kennedy's boyfriend, Josh got arrested and was taken to Albemarle District Jail. While Josh was incarcerated he became acquainted with a few guys. Josh tried to play match maker and wanted to introduce Kassidy to one of the guys in jail. One day when Kennedy went to visit Josh, she took Kassidy with her to meet Josh's new friend.

The guy was very handsome but he wasn't Kassidy's type. At the time Kassidy's cousin was also in jail and he came to the visitation room for a visit and when he saw Kassidy, he asked who she was visiting. Kassidy told him and her cousin responded, "Oh no! I know you can do better than that." Kassidy respected her cousin's opinion very much and she decided that she wasn't going to give the guy a chance. Kassie wouldn't respond to any of the letters that Josh friend sent.

Kassidy had finally finished the first semester which was her last semester of high school. Kassidy continued to work at her uncle's beauty salon full time until graduation came that upcoming spring. April 10th 2001 was Kassidy's 18th birthday and she was excited to make that transition to an adult. Kassie got her license on her birthday. Kassie didn't have a car yet but she would drive her sister, Kennedy's car or her uncle's car when she needed to go somewhere. Kassidy didn't go to the club's as much as she did before, because she was busy focusing on deciding what college she wanted to attend after she graduated.

Kassidy, Kennedy and their mom, Deborah was at a restaurant one evening and a pastor came in to pick up his order for takeout. He spotted Kassie's mother and went over to speak to them. While the pastor was talking to Kassie's mom, Deborah informed him that Kassie was about to graduate high school soon and that she was deciding on what colleges to attend. He asked Kassie, "What schools have you considered and what degree do you want to pursue?" Kassie said, "I will probably go to College of the Albemarle for Office Systems Technology." The minister gave Kassie a stern look and said, "Why limit yourself, when I see so much more potential in you? Don't ever doubt yourself and never settle for less. You need to go to a four year university so that you can have a better opportunity to make more money."

Kassidy took heed to what the minister said and decided that she would apply to a four year university. Those encouraging words from the minister gave Kassidy confidence that she would make it in a four year school. Kassidy also thought about going in the Army reserve, would be a great career. So she met with an army recruiter named Sergeant Brooks.

Sgt. Brooks talked to Kassidy about going in the Army full time or as a reserve. He discussed with Kassie the entire process and the benefits of both programs. Kassie talked to her mother and father about it, and asked for their opinions on what she should do. Deborah wasn't so happy about the idea because she didn't want Kassidy to be far away from her. But Henry on the other hand, was excited about the idea. Henry had been in the Army Reserve and the National Guard, so he definitely wanted Kassie to follow his footsteps.

Sgt. Brooks and Kassie had gone over all the required paperwork and testing that was needed to begin the process. He scheduled a trip for Kassidy to go and tour a local military base. It was an exciting and scary experience for Kassie, because Kassidy still wasn't sure if this was something that she really wanted to do.

Sgt. Brooks scheduled Kassidy an appointment at the MEPS (Military Entrance Processing Station) in Raleigh, NC. He drove Kassidy to the MEPS himself. When they arrive at the MEPS at 8:00 am, Kassidy saw hundreds of young adults there to be processed as well. Everyone had to stand in line until their name was called. This process took all day to complete because there were so many enlistees' and the process was very thorough. At the MEPS, Kassie had to get a complete physical, finger printed, and perform her initial swearing in.

When you enter the military you have to swear in twice. You can back out of it after the initial swear in, but once you have been sworn in the second time, you are in the military until you are discharged. Being sworn in was just like signing a contract. After the MEPS, Kassie started physical training because she knew that she had to be a certain weight and in shape if she wanted to be accepted in the military. Kassie lost a lot of weight and she was proud of herself for doing so.

CHAPTER 7

THE CHASE

One evening, Kassie was sitting at home watching television and she saw a car light flash at the window so she looked outside. There was a black Dodge Neon sitting across the street from Kassie's house. It looked as if they were lost. Then Kassie noticed that the car turned around and drove in her driveway. A young man got out of the car and knocked on the door.

Kassie opened the door to see who it was and it was the guy that she had visited in jail. He said, "Hey Kassidy, can you show me where Josh lives?" Kassie said, "Sure." Apparently he told Josh that he would come visit him once he was released from jail. When Kassie walked outside, there were three guys in the car. The driver of the car insisted that Kassie sit on the front seat with him.

Kassie got in the car and the driver said, "Hello, how are you?" Kassie responded, "I'm fine." Then he asked, "What's your name?" She responded, "Kassidy." He then stated, "My name is Troy." Kassie directed Troy to Josh's house and knocked on the door to see if he was home. Josh's grandfather informed Kassie that he wasn't home and Kassie told him to tell Josh that she stopped by. Kassie got back in the car and Troy began to flirt with her but Kassie just ignored him. Kassie was so sure that Troy was trying to impress the other guys in the car. Troy was irritating Kassie because he seemed to be very arrogant and was full of himself. That was a big turn off for her.

When they arrived to Kassie's house, Troy asked for Kassie's phone number. Usually Kassie wouldn't give guys her number if she wasn't interested, but for some reason she gave Troy her number. Honestly, Kassie didn't think he would call. Kassie thought that he was trying to prove to his friends that he could get her number.

The next day, Kassidy and Kennedy came home from hanging out with their friends and Kassie's mom said, "A guy name Troy called." Kassie checked the caller I.D. so that she could see what number he was calling from. Troy called again later that evening, and again and again. Kassie told her mother to tell Troy that she was out with her friends. This went on for a few weeks. Every day Troy would call Kassie's house and she thought he would give up after a while, but he didn't.

One day Kassie came home and she noticed her mom was on the phone. Kassie asked Deborah, "Who is that?' Deborah put Troy on hold said to Kassie, "I'm talking to Troy and he wants to talk to you." Kassie said, "Tell him I am not here." For almost a week, Troy would call and talk to Deborah for hours at a time.

Kassie became curious to know what her mom and Troy were

talking about for all those hours, so she asked Deborah. Deborah told Kassie that he talked about his job, his daughter, and his family. After a while, Kassidy realized that Troy wasn't going to stop calling until she talked to him. So when Troy called again, Kassie talked to him.

Kassie found out that Troy was easy to talk to and they talked about everything. Kassie told Troy that she did not want to get into a relationship at the moment because she had just got out of a draining relationship. But, Troy was very persistent and he wouldn't take no for an answer. This caught Kassie's attention and she wanted to get to know him more. Troy started calling Kassie every day and the more she talked to him, the more that she liked him and wanted to spend time with him.

Troy was quite a character and Kassie always liked a person who could make her laugh. Troy would sing to Kassie on the phone and she thought that was so cute and sweet. One day he asked Kassie if he could visit her and maybe take her out on a date and Kassie agreed. Kassie couldn't remember what he looked like because she hadn't seen him since the night they first met. Kassie didn't get a good look at him because it was dark and she wasn't really interested in him at the time.

Troy came to visit Kassie one Friday night and she was very nervous. Kassie didn't know what to expect and wasn't sure if she would be attracted to Troy physically. When Troy arrived to Kassie's home, he got out of the car and came to the door. Kassie opened the door, and greeted Troy with a hug. Kassie thought Troy was very handsome, and they left for their date. Troy drove Kassie to his hometown in Elizabeth City, NC.

Troy took Kassie to his home where he stayed with his mother. They talked a lot that night. When Troy's mother came home, he introduced Kassie to his mom. Kassie and Troy soon left his mom's house after they ate dinner. Troy drove Kassie back home and kissed her goodnight. When Kassie walked in her house, her mom asked how her night was. Kassie said, "Ma, I think I'm in love!" Deborah laughed at Kassie and asked, "Already?" Kassie said, "No, but I really like him a lot."

The next day Troy called Kassie and they talked for hours. Troy said that he had a great time and that he wanted to see Kassie again. So Troy came to visit Kassie during the weekend and took her out. This was the first time that Kassie was intimate with Troy.

After Troy took Kassie home, Troy left. Kassie began to wonder if she made a mistake in being intimate with Troy so soon. She wasn't sure if she would hear from Troy anymore after that. But later that night, Troy called Kassie and said, "If you get pregnant, I will be there for you and the baby." Kassie was shocked because she wasn't expecting a call from him, not to mention the statement that he made. That is when Kassie realized Troy was looking to be a part of her life for a while.

They continued to see each other and spend a lot of time together.

Troy introduced Kassie to his family and friends. During this time Kassie had been working at the local Army recruiter's office as a secretary every month. Her job description was to answer the phone and take messages and assist the officers with recruiting other applicants into the military.

When Troy found out Kassie was planning to go into the military, he became upset. He didn't want her to leave him because they were becoming so close. As time went on, Kassie began to second guess herself about her decision to leave for basic training and wondered if it was something that she really wanted to do or was she doing it to please others. Kassie soon realized that entering the military was not something that she wanted for her life, and it wasn't her dream. Kassie started missing her appointments with Sgt. Brooks and not answering his phone calls. With graduation and the date for Kassie to leave to go to basic training quickly approaching, she still wasn't sure what she wanted to do.

CHAPTER 8

ONE FOR THE FATHER

Henry decided to sell the home and property that Kassie and her family had lived on for the last 13 years. Kassie started jumping from one friend's house to the next trying to figure out where she was going to live. While staying with one of her friends, Kassie suddenly became ill. So she scheduled an appointment with her doctor for the following day.

Troy went with Kassie to the doctor's appointment because he was very concerned. After running a few tests, the doctor informed Kassie that she had a bladder infection. Kassie was relieved that it wasn't anything serious or something that was incurable, so Kassie didn't think it was a big deal. She went to the pharmacy and got her prescription and started taking her medication. Once Kassie symptoms ceased, she stopped taking the prescription.

That next week, Kassie spent as few nights with one of her friends from high school because they had to go to her Baccalaureate program. Kassie talked to her friend a lot about her relationship with Troy. Kassie told her that she really could see herself having a future with him.

Later that night, Kassie started feeling really bad. She was experiencing some excruciating back pains in her lower back. Kassie tried to take a nap hoping that maybe she would feel better, but the pain just wouldn't go away. So Kassie asked her friend if she could take her to the emergency room at the hospital. Kassie told her friend that there was a possibility that she could be pregnant. Kassie's friend told her not to think about it until she had proof.

Kassie arrive at the hospital around 12:00 am midnight on May 24th of 2001. Kassie's pains had intensified so much that she couldn't even sit down. The nurse called Kassie back to the triage room and they began to ask her questions as they evaluated her. Kassie told them about her infection and that she didn't complete the dosage of medication. The nurses took blood and urine samples for testing to see what was causing Kassie so much pain. They gave her pain medication which caused her to relax and sleep.

When the doctor came in, he said, "The pain that you are experiencing is because you didn't finish your prescription. Since you didn't finish your prescription, now the infection has spread to your kidneys." Kassie blamed herself because she knew it was her own fault that she was in so much pain. If Kassie had finished the dosage as prescribed, the infection would not have spread to her kidneys.

The doctor continued, "So we are going to admit you in the hospital for a couple hours, give you an IV and monitor you." Kassidy replied, "Wow, this really must be a serious infection, because I've never heard of anyone having to be admitted in the hospital for a kidney infection." Kassidy was confused and concerned at the same time. Graduation was the next day and she didn't want to miss that for anything in the world.

The doctor left to ensure that the physicians were preparing for Kassie's arrival on the second floor. Kassie continued to lie in bed and there was a curtain that separated each patient from the other. As Kassie was lying on the bed, she heard the nurse ask the doctor, "What did Ms. Bell say?" The doctor asked, "About what?" The nurse responded, "Oh my God, you didn't tell her?"

Then the doctor and the nurse pulled back the curtain and approached Kassie. They startled Kassie and she sat up on the bed. Worried that they were about to give her bad news, Kassie asked, "Is there something wrong?" The doctor said, "Ms. Bell, your blood work and urine tests determined that you are pregnant." Kassie sat there with her mouth wide open. Kassie had an inkling that she was pregnant, but to actually hear it come out of the doctor's mouth, stunned her.

The nurse explained to Kassie that she had to be hospitalized and be treated because she was pregnant, if she wasn't pregnant they could have treated her infection as an outpatient. Kassie's friend came to visit her and to ask how Kassie was. Kassie told her that she had a kidney infection and that she was also pregnant. Kassie's friend stated, "Oh my God, you were just telling me that you thought you could be pregnant." Kassidy asked her friend to call her mom and inform her that she had to be admitted in the hospital.

Deborah arrived at the hospital and she chastised Kassidy for not completing her prescription. She said, "You wouldn't be in this mess if you had taken the entire prescription." Kassie said, "I know mom." Kassie immediately assumed that her mother knew that she was pregnant. So Kassie said, "Now I have someone else to think about other than myself." Deborah asked, "What are you talking about Kassie?" Kassie said, "The baby, mom." Deborah asked, "What baby are you talking about?" Kassie responded, "My baby. I'm pregnant." The look on Deborah's face, showed the disappointment that she was feeling at that moment. Kassidy was so sure that her friend had told her mom everything, but she didn't. Kassie was finally moved upstairs to her room and her mom called their family and friends to let them know how Kassie was doing.

Kassie thought about Troy and wondered how he would react to the news. Troy had previously talked about having children with Kassie but she was still uncertain of his reaction to the news. Kassie called Troy around 2:00 am but he didn't answer. When Troy woke up he noticed the missed call so he called the number back. Kassie picked up the phone, and Troy immediately recognized her voice and asked, "What's wrong?" Kassie informed Troy about being hospitalized for a kidney infection and the baby.

Troy became quiet and he didn't respond immediately. Kassie asked, "Are you okay?" Troy responded, "Yes, I'm just in shock." Troy had to prepare for work so he told Kassie that he loved her and that he would call her on his lunch break.

Later that day, some of Kassie's family and friends came to visit her. Kassie asked the nurse when she would be released from the hospital. She expressed her concerns about wanting to attend her high school graduation rehearsal which was in a few hours. The nurse made Kassie a promise that she would be discharged before graduation rehearsal. The hospital prepared Kassie's discharge papers and released her.

Kassie's class rehearsed outside on the football field but there was a chance that it would rain that night and that they might have to have their graduation inside. The following day which was May 25th, 2001, which was graduation day. Kassie was so excited and ready to end that chapter of her life. Troy told Kassie that he would try to leave work early so that he could make it to her graduation.

During the ceremony, Kassie was excited and nervous, but not so much about graduation. She was nervous and excited about becoming a mother for the first time and she wondered what her life would be like. Kassie walked across the stage and received her diploma, and Kassie's family cheered for her. That was an amazing feeling for Kassidy and she was happy to complete that journey.

After the ceremony, Kassie sister Kennedy took her to their church where their family were waiting to surprise Kassie with a graduation celebration. When Kassie arrived to her church, some of her friends and family were there. They ate, laughed and gave Kassie presents.

Deborah approached Kassie and said, "You have a visitor outside." Kassie went outside and Troy was standing there waiting for her. They hugged and kissed, and Kassie was so excited that Troy came to celebrate with her. When the party was over, Kassie and her friends were planning to attend the Afram Festival in Norfolk, Virginia that weekend to continue their graduation celebration. So Kassie gathered her bags and went to her friend's house, where everyone was meeting to leave. While everyone was putting their bags in the car, Kassie kissed Troy goodbye.

Kassie and her friends drove to Virginia and checked in to their rooms at the hotel. That weekend was great, it was fun and exciting. Kassie and her friends went to a concert on Saturday where they saw famous singer's Carl Thomas and Ray J. After they left the festival, Kassie and her friends did a little shopping in Downtown Norfolk. The next day they spent most of their day at the beach. They had a great time laughing, taking pictures, and just enjoying their time together before they went their separate ways in life.

The weekend was over and they drove back home. When Kassie got home, reality set in. She started thinking about her future plans especially since she was about to become a mother. Kassie knew that the military was out of the question, because she didn't want to leave her baby. Kassie started applying for jobs in Elizabeth City, NC because she wanted to attend Elizabeth City State University. Kassie wasn't sure about what major she was going to choose, but she knew that ECSU was a definite decision. She eventually landed a job as a dietary aide at Winslow's Memorial which is a nursing home in Elizabeth City. The job only paid minimum wage, but it was a start.

Troy and Kassie started discussing their future together since they were starting a family. They talked about getting an apartment together, so they applied at several apartment complexes. Troy's mom knew that Kassie would be working in the area so she offered to let Kassie move in with her and Troy until their got our own place. Kassie packed up her belongings and moved in with Troy and his mom. Kassie and Troy's mom had become very close, she really loved Kassie and she showed it too. Kassie loved Troy's mom too and Troy's mom would often call Kassie her daughter.

CHAPTER 9

TRUE COLORS

Kassie knew it was time to tell her recruiter that she was not going to leave for basic training because she was pregnant. But Kassie didn't know how to tell Sgt. Brooks. One morning Sgt. Brooks called Kassie to do PT (Physical Training). Kassie told Sgt. Brooks, "I won't be able to do PT and I need to talk to you about something." Kassie informed Sgt. Brooks about her pregnancy and her decision not to join the military. Sgt. Brooks asked, "What are your plans? Are you keeping the baby?" Kassie responded, "Yes, I'm keeping the baby. Abortion is not an option!"

He said, "You can still have the baby and then join the military after the baby is born. The only thing is you will have to sign over your rights to your mother until you are released from the military.." Kassie said, "That's not happening either! I conceived this child, therefore I'm going to raise my child. I will not put my responsibility on anybody else. I will just have to find another way to make it."

Sgt. Brooks was disappointed at Kassie because he had helped her through the entire process and got her to the point where she was just waiting to leave for basic training. But God had another plan for Kassie's life. Kassie felt bad because she knew she disappointed Sgt. Brooks and she apologized to him.

She informed her father that she was not going into the military and he was very disappointed in her. Henry asked Kassidy what changed her mind about joining the military and she told him that she was pregnant. Henry said, "Oh now I see why you don't want to go into the military." Kassie could tell by his voice that he wasn't happy, but it was her life and she was determined not to live her life for anybody but herself and her unborn child.

Kassie began working at the nursing home and she continued to apply for apartments for her, Troy and the baby. Kassidy didn't have a car but she would catch rides with her family and friends. Sometimes Kassie had to call a cab to go to work or get to her appointments. Kassie went to the Department of Social Services and applied for food stamps, WIC, and Medicaid. Kassie wasn't too proud not to apply for welfare because she knew she needed help but she was determined that she wasn't going to depend on it forever.

One day Troy's mom and Kassie where home alone and she said to Kassie, "When I first met you, I wasn't sure about you." Kassie asked, "Why not?" She responded, "It wasn't that I didn't like you but I thought that you were going to be another random girl that Troy would date. But it looks like you're going to be around for a while." She told Kassie that Troy was a "Playboy" and loved women, so she didn't think he was ready to settle down.

She then began to tell Kassie about some of Troy's past relationships with females that he used to talk to. Kassie was surprised at what Troy's mom was telling her because he treated Kassie like a queen and made her feel special. So for Kassie to hear this coming from Troy's mother was unreal.

Troy's mom also informed Kassie that the car he was driving when they first met, the car that he drove on their first date, and the car that he drove to see Kassie after graduation which was the Dodge Neon, was not Troy's car. Kassie said to Troy's mom, "Troy told me that you bought the car for him." Troy's mom responded, "No, I didn't. That's one of the females that he use to date car."

Kassie became angry with Troy for lying to her. She felt like their relationship had been based on a lie. Everything that Troy had told Kassidy was not true. Kassie thought about walking away from Troy and their relationship, but she loved Troy so much and now was carrying his child so she decided to stick it out. Kassidy tried to rationalize it by convincing herself that maybe Troy lied to her to impress her not knowing that he would actually catch feelings for her.

That evening when Troy arrived home from work, Kassie confronted him about what his mother told her. Troy admitted to everything that he lied about. He told Kassie, "As soon as we started dating, I broke it off with her but she was still allowing me to drive her car." Kassie was disappointed and it was their first argument as a couple, but eventually she got over it. Troy had a way about him, where he could charm Kassie to believe whatever he said and do just about anything he wanted. So Kassie forgave him.

Every time Troy would take Kassie to visit his aunts and grandmother, Troy would tell them that he was going to marry Kassie one day. His aunts would respond, "Girl, what have you done to my nephew? He has never talked about marrying anyone or settling down before." Kassie would smile because that was definitely something that she wanted to hear and wanted for her family. Kassie and Troy stayed with his mother for about a month and a half before they received a call from Southgate Manor Apartments. Kassie was so excited because they were finally going to be on their own and in their own place. Nothing meant more to Kassie than to have her own apartment before her child was born.

They moved into a two bedroom apartment and the only furniture that they had was a queen size bed that Troy's mother bought them and a television. Kassie continued to work at the nursing home and she made quite a few friends on the job. Some of Kassie's co-workers would alternate to take her to work and drop her off to her home. Sometimes Kassie's co-workers would even take her to her appointments.

Kassie and Troy hadn't saved enough money to buy a car yet so they had to do what they needed to get from point A to B. When Kassie went to her 4 month appointment, the doctor told her that she was having a boy. Kassie was excited because she and Troy wanted a son especially since he already had a daughter that was five years old at the time. As time passed, Kassie stomach grew bigger and she began to feel her baby moving in her belly. That was an amazing feeling for Kassie because she had never experienced anything like that before.

Kassie and Troy was starting to get overwhelmed with bills, having to pay rent, and not having their own transportation. They were barely making ends meet. Kassie and Troy needed more furniture so Kassie's mom offered to let them have a few dressers and her kitchen table set from her home. One night Kassie went to her mom's house to get the items and Troy stayed home. Kassie spent most of that day in Tyner with her mom and family since she hadn't seen much of them lately. Later that night Kassie's cousins took her back home with the kitchen table and dressers. Kassie's cousin's helped take the items in her apartment for her and they left.

Troy was home but Kassie figured that he was sleeping because he didn't come downstairs to speak to her when she arrived. Kassie went upstairs and she noticed Troy lying on the bed. She went to the bathroom to get ready for bed and when she walked in the bedroom to lie down, Troy got up and walked in the bathroom. Kassie looked at Troy strangely because he walked right past her and didn't say a word. When he walked back in the bedroom, Troy jumped on top of Kassie. Kassie thought Troy was playing with her at first but then she realized that he was serious. Kassie asked, "What's wrong with you?"

Then Troy sat on top of Kassie's chest with his knees on top of her arms holding them down and he started slapping Kassie in her face. Kassie started having a panic attack because she was restrained and was having a hard time breathing.

In a second Troy had snapped and Kassie thought he was going to kill her. As Troy slapped Kassie in the face he asked her, "Why are you writing him?" Kassie asked, "I don't know what you're talking about?" Troy responded, "Kent. While you were gone, I found the letter in the trash can that you started writing to him." Kassie then realized what made Troy so upset.

One day when Troy was working Kassie started to write Kent a letter because he was constantly asking her mother about her. Kassie decided to write Kent to inform him about her relationship with Troy and to tell him that she didn't think it was a good idea to try to contact her anymore. Although Kassie and Kent were no longer together, Kassie felt obligated to tell him about her relationship with Troy and about her baby that was on the way. But Kassie never got the chance to finish the letter. Kassie only wrote the greeting of the letter which said; "Dear Kent" then she tore the letter up and threw it in the trash. That is where Troy found it.

Kassie began to cry and continued to tell Troy that she loved him and that she wanted to be with him. Finally, Troy got off of Kassidy chest. Kassie began rubbing her stomach because she was afraid that it had caused stress and harm to the baby. Kassie was almost 5 ½ months at the time and she wasn't sure if the baby was ok or not. When Kassie looked into Troy's eyes, there was a coldness about them. Kassie could tell that he had been drinking because there was a bottle by the bed and the smell of alcohol was seeping through his skin. It took Kassie a while to get herself together because Troy had never treated her that way before and she was in a state of shock.

Kassie began to feel weak emotionally. She had always seen herself as a strong young lady who wasn't going to take any type of abuse from anybody. Kassie had always pride herself as a strong woman with a mind of her own. She used to say that she would never allow a man to put his hands on her nor would she ever be a victim of abuse. But that is what she had become, a VICTIM.

Unknowingly, Kassie was beginning to lose herself in the relationship, and everything that she once stood for went out of the window. Kassie figured if she loved him enough and prayed hard enough that Troy would change and be the man that she needed him to be. Kassie knew that she should have left him, but she thought that if she had never wrote the letter to Kent that Troy wouldn't have become so jealous. Kassie tried to justify his reaction, so she stayed. Kassie eventually forgave Troy for that incident and he promised her that it would never happen again.

But Kassie still needed to know where all of that anger that Troy displayed, originated from. Although Kassie was young, she was mature enough to know that there was always a root to why people behaved the way that they did. So she contacted Troy's sister Sherry. Kassie told Sherry about Troy's aggressive behaviors the night before and asked her if he always acted that way.

Sherry told Kassie that when Troy was younger, he saw his mother and father fight a lot. Sherry also told Kassie that his mother abused alcohol and that his father abused narcotics and when his father would get angry he would take his frustrations out on his mother. Kassie felt sorry for Troy and wanted so much to help Troy and give him the love that she thought he needed.

CHAPTER 10

THE CHRISTMAS PRESENT

It was Thanksgiving and Kassie had requested that day off from work because Thanksgiving was her favorite holiday. Kassidy wanted to spend time with her family and Troy, but Troy had other plans. Troy left the apartment early that morning and said that he would come back to take Kassie to his family's house for Thanksgiving dinner. Later that afternoon, Kassie got ready for the day and put her clothes on. Kassie tried calling Troy several times so that he could come get her, but he would never return her phone calls. Kassie was annoyed and frustrated with Troy because she was getting very hungry. Troy had left her in the house with no money, no food and no transportation. Kassie thought to herself, "How could he leave me like this alone?"

Kassie walked to her job which was about a mile away from where she lived to get out of the house and see a few of her co-workers. Kassie visited her co-workers for almost an hour and decided that she would go back home. Kassie got a friend of hers to take her home.

Finally after hours of waiting, Troy showed up at the apartment with his a few of his friends. It was about 7:30 pm when he arrived and Kassie was infuriated. Troy didn't bring any food back for Kassie and he told her that he had been with his family. Kassie told him that she had been waiting for him all day and reminded Troy that he told her he would come back to pick her up. Since Troy didn't bring Kassie any food, he sent her with his friend's car to get some food from his cousin's house.

Kassie took the keys and got in the car and cried all the way to Troy's cousin's house. She was embarrassed and hurt at the way Troy was treating her. After Kassie got her plate, she drove to an empty parking lot where she ate her food. She was too upset to go back to the apartment around Troy and his friends just yet. Once Kassie got herself together, she went home.

Things did not get better between Kassie and Troy. As a matter of fact, women started calling the apartment for Troy and he was showing Kassie a different side of him. Troy started showing Kassie the man that his mother had described to her, the man that she never thought she would see. Troy started taking showers late at night, and he would get dressed and put on cologne and wait for Kassie to get home.

Once Kassie was home, Troy would leave and go to his friend's apartment and stay out all night. Kassie didn't want to be a nagging girlfriend, so she gave Troy some space to hang out with friends. But then it became an every night thing.

One night Kassie watched Troy leave to go to his friend's apartment. Troy's friend lived in the same apartment complex. After a few minutes

Kassie saw two cars arrive in the parking lot and several females entered into Troy's friend's apartment. Kassie realized why Troy was getting dressed at night to go to his friend's house because he was meeting women there. It explained why Troy would come home early the next morning. Kassie knew at this point that she and Troy had serious problems. Kassie confronted Troy about the late nights and the women that she saw entering his friend's apartment, but Troy denied any allegations of being disloyal and said that he only went over there to talk to his friend. Kassie found this hard to believe.

Christmas was approaching and Kassie didn't have the money to buy any Christmas presents. Kassie continued to work at the nursing home and Troy continued to work at the Insulation Company where he worked when they first met. One day Kassie's co-worker, Nita asked her to spend the day with, so she agreed. Kassie figured getting out of the house would do her some good, especially with everything that she had been going through lately.

So she went with Nita as she paid her bills, then they got some lunch and had a relaxing day. They went to Nita's house to rest because Kassie was very much pregnant at the time. Kassie slept for about two hours and when she woke up, she overheard Nita talking to someone on the phone.

Kassie heard Nita say something about a baby shower but she was still semi-conscious, so she just brushed it off. About 8 o'clock that evening Nita said, "Okay, let's stop by Nett's house (which was another co-worker) to see what's she is up to." Kassie said, "Okay." Kassie was so tired and really wanted to go home at this point but she went along with it anyway. When they arrive to Nett's house, Nita knocked on the door. Nett said, "Come in, it's open." Nita insisted that Kassie went in first, so she opened the door. To Kassie's surprise, it was a baby shower just for her. All of Kassie's co-workers were there and Deborah, Kennedy and Khloe were invited also.

Kassie immediately started crying, she couldn't believe that they planned her shower without her having a clue of what was going on. Kassie could feel the love and support from her family and friends which was what she really needed. Kassie got all the things that she needed for the baby and she didn't have to buy anything. She was blessed tremendously. Kassie took everything home and Troy was there to help her unpack all the items.

The following week, Kassie started folding the baby clothes and putting them in drawers in preparation for the baby's arrival. Kassie received a call from Kennedy that night and they talked for almost an hour. At the end of their conversation, Troy walked in and heard Kassie tell Kennedy that her neighbor wanted her to tell Kennedy that he said hello. When Kassie ended the call, Troy grabbed Kassie by the hair and pulled her upstairs. Kassie screamed to Troy, "What's are you doing?" Troy responded, "Why were you talking to that dude? You better not talk to him again." Kassie replied, "What are you talking about? All I did was speak to him and he wanted me to tell Kennedy that he said hello. That is all we said to each other."

Kassie and Troy got into a push and shove match that night, which caused much stressed to Kassie and the baby. Troy "man handled" Kassie like he didn't care that she was pregnant with his child. Kassie asked Troy, "I thought you said you weren't going to hurt me again?" Troy began to call Kassie every names in the book from "Slut, bitch, tramp, and whore." If you can name it, he said it.

After the fight, Kassie was so exhausted she fell asleep. Troy woke up the next morning and went to work like nothing ever happened.

The next morning, Kassie woke up around 9:00 am with sharp pains in her stomach and back. She laid in bed for a while hoping that the pains would go away, but they didn't. Kassie called her mom and told her about the pains that she was feeling. Deborah became very concerned because Kassie wasn't due until January 25th 2002. Deborah told Kassie, "Well if it gets worse, ask someone to take you to the emergency room." About 40 minutes later the pains increased, they were coming closer together and Kassie couldn't bare them anymore so she called Nita and asked her to take her to the hospital.

When Kassie got to the hospital, the doctor's evaluated her. He told Kassie, "Ms. Bell, you are six centimeters dilated and it looks like your baby is coming today." Nita called Kassie's job and informed them that Kassie would not be able to work the evening shift later that day so that they could find her replacement. Kassie called her mom and informed her of what was going on and she asked her mom, "Can you come to the hospital to be with me?" Deborah replied, "I'm on my way, Kassie. I wouldn't miss this for nothing in the world." Once Kassie's mom got to the hospital, Nita left because she had to go to work. Kassie was only in labor for about 9 hours.

At 5:52 p.m. on December 12th, 2001, Kassie gave birth to her first child weighing at 4 lbs., 9 oz. Kassie named her son Kevin. Kevin was a born prematurely as a result of the fight that she and Troy had the night before. Since Kevin was premature, his lungs were undeveloped. Therefore the Hospital sent him to Children's Hospital of the King's Daughters in Norfolk, Virginia for neonatal care. Kassie was discharged that next morning and her dad and stepmom took her to CHKD so that she could be with Kevin. Troy stayed home because he had to work, but Kassie left to be with her son.

Henry helped Kassie check in at the Ronald McDonald house so that she could have somewhere to stay while Kevin stayed in the hospital. Henry and Rachael left Kassie to be with Kevin and went home. Kassie stayed with Kevin for the rest of the day. Kassie would have stayed with her son all day if the hospital would have let her, but the nurse would wake Kassie up during their shift change to tell her to leave and get some rest so that she could visit Kevin later.

At first Kassie was stressed out because she wanted to be able to bring her son home from the hospital just like most mothers were able to do. Kassie began to question God, "Why did my son have to be hospitalized? Why couldn't he be healthy enough to come home with me?"

But one day while visiting her son, Kassie saw a couple visiting their daughter. The baby girl was 8 months old and the doctor's wouldn't release her to go home either. A few days later, Kassie saw another baby who was very tiny in size, weighing only about 2 lbs. and she was born addicted to crack cocaine. Kassie started to realize that no matter what her son was going through, that he was still blessed. She realized that his health issues could have been worse. Kassie realized just how fortunate her son was and she asked God for forgiveness for questioning him.

Kevin stayed in the hospital for almost two weeks and Kassie was becoming exhausted. Troy finally asked his cousin to take him to the hospital to see his son, Kevin. Troy seemed very nervous to touch Kevin because he was so small. After Troy visited Kevin for a few hours, Kassie left the hospital with Troy to get some rest and get more items that she needed. That was the first time that Kassie left Kevin's bedside. But

Kassie was exhausted and needed a change of scenery, so she went home that night with plans to return in a few days. When Kassie arrived home she slept for hours.

Christmas was approaching in a few days and Kassie knew since she didn't have a car that she probably wouldn't be able to visit Kevin on Christmas day. So Kassie asked her co-worker Nita to take her to visit Kevin on Christmas Eve. When they arrived to the hospital, Nita held Kevin for the first time. They spent a couple hours with Kevin and then they went back home.

When Kassie got home, she received a phone call from CHKD hospital where Kevin was admitted and the nurse asked, "Is this Ms. Bell? Kassie responded, "Yes." The nurse said, "We were trying to catch you before you left to inform you that we are going to discharge Kevin and you could take him home for good." Kassie screamed with excitement.

Kassie asked, "You're kidding me right?" The nurse laughed and responded, "No ma'am. You can come and pick him up tomorrow if you want to." Kassie thought, "What a blessing it would be to bring my son home on Christmas Day." Kassie immediately called Nita and asked her if she could take her to pick up Kevin. Nita said, "I will be happy to take you." So they left early Christmas morning and went to the hospital.

When they got there, Kevin had to complete a few tests before they could take him home. Once the hospital were done testing Kevin, they discharged him and allowed Kassie to take him home. Kassie was so excited and nervous at the same time. Kassie was finally taking her son home after being hospitalized for two weeks.

When they got back in town Nita had to go to work, so Kassie went home with her son. Troy was at his mom's house and Kassie called him to tell him that she and the baby were home. About thirty minutes later Troy came home and he talked to Kevin all night. That was the best Christmas present that Kassie and Troy could have asked for.

CHAPTER 11

TWO FOR THE SON

After six weeks, Kassie went back to work at the nursing home. She continued to work and things didn't get easier for her. Troy became even more controlling and wanted to know Kassie's whereabouts such as, who was she going with, where she was going, how long would she be there, and etc.

One night Kassie allowed one of her friends to spend the night with them and she slept in the other bedroom. She invited Kassie to go to a party with her. Ever since Kassie gave birth to Kevin, she hadn't had a day to herself and she needed to get out and have some time alone. After all, Troy would hang out all the time leaving Kassie in the house with their son. It's no wonder Kassie was still in her right frame of mind after all she had to deal with.

Troy knew that Kassie wanted to go to the party so he gave her an ultimatum that if she went to the party, that he would leave her. So of course, Kassie went to the party anyway. Ultimatums didn't work with Kassie and she was going to prove it. The party was packed and the music was pumping loud, but Kassie couldn't enjoy herself because all she could think about was Troy. She thought about how much she loved him and wanted to be spending that time with him.

Kassie and her friend left the party and went home. When Kassie got home, Troy was not there and he never came home that evening. Kassie couldn't sleep at all that night. She paced the floor back and forth looking out the window for Troy, but he never came home.

The next morning Kassie's friend left for school and on her way out of the apartment complex, she called Kassie and told her that she saw Troy going to his friend's apartment. Kassie called Troy's friend who lived in the same complex and asked him if Troy was there. But of course, Troy's friend lied to Kassie and said he that he had no clue where Troy was. Kassie knew that Troy's friend wasn't telling her the truth and she continued to call him. After a while Troy's friend stopped answering Kassie's calls. So Kassie decided to leave Troy and she called her father to ask him if she could stay with him for a while until she found a place to stay.

Henry agreed to let Kassie and Kevin stay with them until she figured out what she was going to do next. Kassidy packed up her and Kevin's belongings and moved into her dad's home. While she was gone Troy partied all day and night for several days. After a few days, Troy began missing Kassie and Kevin so he started calling Henry's house. Troy even visited Kassie and Kevin a few times at her dad's house. Troy wanted them to come home with him, but Kassie wasn't sure if that was where she wanted to be. Troy was very persistent and he called Kassie every day until he convinced Kassie to finally go back home.

Troy packed up Kassie and Kevin's belongings and moved them back in the apartment with him. The same day that Kassie moved home, Troy took the sheets and comforter off of the bed to get them cleaned. Immediately Kassie's antennas went up, and she thought that he was trying to cover up something. But Kassie didn't feel like having an argument and she really didn't have any proof, so she kept her thoughts to herself. Kassie and Troy was starting over with a clean slate.

A few weeks later Troy and Kassie were home spending some quality time together with their son when suddenly the phone rang. Kassie answered the phone and it was a female and she wanted to talk to Troy. When Kassie asked the female, "Why?" She told Kassie that she was from Newbern, NC and that she met Troy there over a month ago. She informed Kassie that she spent the weekend with Troy at their apartment, which just happen to be the same weekend Kassie left to stay with her dad.

Kassie didn't believe the woman at first because she knew that women could be vindictive at times. But then the woman began to describe Kassie's apartment to her in detail. Kassie knew then that she wasn't lying to her. She told Kassie what type of feminine hygiene products that Kassie had under her sink. Kassie dropped the phone and begin attacking Troy. She started punching, slapping, kicking and scratching him. Kassie lost her trust in Troy and started to see him in a different light. This drained Kassie emotionally. Kassie knew that it would take her a long time to forgive him for cheating.

Kassie called her co-worker to come pick her up because she needed to get away from the house and Troy. Kassie's friend gave her a cigarette to calm her nerves. She was so stressed out that she smoked two cigarettes one behind the other. Before that moment, Kassie never liked the smell of cigarette smoke and it used to make her sick on the stomach. But Kassie was becoming someone that she didn't know anymore.

Kassie grew tired of not making enough money at her job and now that she had her son, she needed to make more than the minimum wage. Kassie asked her stepmother to help her get a job where she was working at Food Lion. Kassie's stepmom worked in Southern Shores, NC where there were better opportunities to make more money than Elizabeth City, NC. So Kassie left Winslow's and started working at Food Lion as a cashier.

Even though Kassie was making more money, she knew that it wasn't where she wanted to be forever. Kassie always wanted more for her future. Kassie had almost forgot about her dreams of furthering her education because she was so caught up with life. She started thinking about school again and what she wanted to major in. So she went to Elizabeth City State University to enroll for fall classes. Kassie was so excited and was happy that she was making progress towards her future. She was determined that she was not going to let her son down by becoming a statistic of having a child and not providing a better life for him. Kassie wanted to be someone that her son could be proud of. Kassie continued to work five days a week and eight hours shifts. She hated the hours but she loved that she was making more money than before.

However, Kassie was still on welfare such as food stamps, Medicaid, WIC and EIC. But Kassie's plan was not to depend on the government forever. Every time Kassie had an appointment with her welfare case worker, she would make Kassie feel guilty for needing assistance. This made Kassie very angry because she was only there because she needed to be.

Kassie and Troy continued to have problems in their relationship and her friends and family would tell her often, "Whatever you do please don't have another baby by him because if you are having problems with him now, you are going to have more problems with two children."

When Kassie worked at Food Lion, she stayed to herself. Kassie was really a friendly person but she would never put herself on anyone, especially people that she didn't know. Kassie's motto was, "What you see is what you get." If someone didn't like Kassie, she wouldn't allow it to affect her. She was a person who didn't allow people to define her. Kassie would have to warm up to someone and get to know that person before she would allow them in her circle. Trust was not something that Kassie gave to everybody. Trust would have to be earned to be in Kassie's circle and trust must be maintained to stay there.

So Kassie mostly worked hard and she never tried to make friends because she knew she had a job to do. It wasn't a surprise to Kassie that the person who helped her get the job, gave her the hardest time on the job, her stepmom. Rachael would talk about Kassie to their co-workers and the co-workers would later tell Kassie what Rachael said about her. Kassie knew that she couldn't trust Rachael. Rachael was one of those people that you had to feed with a long handle spoon.

At home Kassie would "spaz out" from time to time for no reason. At first Kassie thought that maybe she was just under a lot of stress from becoming a new mother and Troy and her were having problems. Kassie moods were changing frequently but she couldn't understand why.

One minute Kassie was happy, the next minute she was angry and then she would burst into tears. Kassie couldn't understand what was going on with her until she remembered that the last time she felt that way was when she was pregnant with Kevin. Kassie thought to herself, "This cannot be happening again. I can't be pregnant!" Kassie called Troy that night after she got to work and told him about how her mood was fluctuating and that she thought she could be pregnant again. Troy told Kassie, "Maybe you should take a pregnancy test just to be sure."

That night when Kassie got off from work, she purchased a

pregnancy test. When she got home she took the test and immediately two lines displayed on the test. Kassie was pregnant again. Kassie started crying hysterically and she called Troy and informed him. Troy was so happy but Kassie had mixed emotions about it. There was so much running through her mind such as, "How can we make it with two children, when we are already struggling with one?"

Kassie then remembered what her family and friends told her about not having another child because of what she was already going through with Troy. Kassie thought about school and wondered, "How can I go to school with two babies?" Kassie felt like she was failing her future and her family. She was becoming a statistic and that was something that she always said she would never be.

Kassie called her mom and she was crying on the phone when her mom answered. Deborah asked, "Baby what's wrong?" Kassie said, "I have something to tell you. I'm pregnant!" Deborah responded, "Okay, so why are you crying?" Kassie rambled nervously, "I know you are disappointed in me because I am having another baby so soon. Kevin isn't even 6 months old yet and now I won't be able to go to school with two babies."

Deborah replied, "Kassie if you don't go to school and graduate, it won't be because you can't do it but it will be because deep down you really don't want to." Deborah then stated, "I have seen so many women go to college with two or three children and still graduate. So don't use that as an excuse not to go."

After Kassie's talk with her mother, she dried her face and decided to "suck it up." Those words of encouragement from her mom motivated Kassie to go to school and further her education. Kassie told the rest of her family that she was having another baby and about her decision to go to college while being pregnant. Some of Kassie's family didn't believe that she was serious about school. They doubted her determination and motivation. Some of Kassie's family were supportive and encouraged her to complete her journey with school.

But when Kassie told her father and step-mother, Rachael said something to Kassie that she would never forget. She told Kassie, "As long as you are with Troy, you will never finish college." There was one thing about Kassie that Rachael didn't know and it was that Kassie had sheer determination. Kassie's biggest motivation kicked in when someone would tell her what she couldn't do.

CHAPTER 12

COLLEGE

Kassidy began attending classes in the fall of 2002. She was 3 months pregnant with her second child and her son Kevin was now 8 months old. Kassie's friends took turns taking her to school the first semester because she still didn't have any transportation.

Kassie got hired as a cashier at Captain D's in Elizabeth City, NC which was much closer to home than working at Food Lion at the beach, especially since she didn't have transportation. Captain D's was located directly behind her apartment complex, so Kassidy could walked to work most of the time. Kassie was so dedicated to her job that she even walk in the rain, sleet and snow while being pregnant. Sometimes Kassie had to work the night shift and it was not very often that someone would offer to give her a ride home from work. Kassie was so anxious to get her own transportation so she wouldn't have to depend on anyone.

Kassidy went to school her first semester and she did well with her classes. Kassie was so ready for that semester to be over because she had to walk across the campus to all of her classes. This was very difficult for Kassie to do with a big stomach and a heavy book bag to carry around.

During Kassie's first semester, Troy did not try to make life easy for Kassie at all. Women were calling the apartment and Kassie's cell phone asking to speak to Troy. Things got so bad between them that Troy decided to move out of their apartment and began staying with his mother.

Kassie had a Monday night Biology class and sometimes she had to take a cab to and from class. There were nights when Troy wouldn't watch Kevin so that Kassie could attend class. So Kassie had to take Kevin with her to her night class in a cab. She would carry Kevin in his carrier, holding her books in the other hand, while her second child was growing inside of her. Kassie was determined that nothing was going to stop her from achieving her goal, not even Troy.

This was not easy for Kassie because she still had to make sure that she wasn't putting too much strain on her unborn baby. Some of Kassie's classmates felt sorry for her, so they decided to take turns taking her back and forth to class. Kassie thought that Troy would be happy for her and encourage her to go to school but instead he did everything in his power to keep her from achieving her goal.

Kassie believed that Troy wanted to keep her limited so that he could maintain control over her. Troy tried everything that he could to break Kassie, but it only pushed Kassie harder and made her more determined to complete that journey. Kassie knew that she had to finish school, so that she could have a better opportunity at life. Kassie felt like she didn't have a choice whether not to finish school and giving up was not an option for her. She would constantly remind herself, "If I don't finish school, I will have to work two or three jobs and struggle for the rest of my life. But if I stay in school, I will only struggle for four years and then be set for life."

Kassie's family in Tyner threw her a baby shower at their church. Kassie's Uncle Sam decorated and cooked all of the food for the shower. The baby shower was really nice and they blessed Kassie unborn son with great gifts. Most of Kassie's church family came to show their love and support and Kassie felt good because that was the support that she needed.

Kassie and her family celebrated Kevin's first birthday and then Christmas together and Kassie's stomach was getting bigger. Kassie's due date was February 9th, 2003. During the Christmas break, Kassie frequently walked in hopes of having her son during the holidays so that she could go back to school in January. However, she didn't want another premature childbirth. Kassie was a little overwhelmed and tired because she had a busy 1 year old at home, she was working, going to school full-time and had another baby on the way. It was a lot for Kassie to handle. Kassie prayed to God a lot asking for strength to continue her journey.

When Kassie returned to school from her winter break, she was still pregnant. Kassie was getting tired and impatient as her stomach grew bigger and bigger. Kassie was glad to be pregnant, however she was ready for it to be over because she had been dealing with so much stress. Some people criticized Kassie because they thought that she was too young to be a mother of two children.

Kassie and Troy's relationship issues only got worse with time and Kassie couldn't put her finger on the reason why. One evening Kassie was waiting for Troy to come home, it had been snowing that day. Kassie was about 8 months at this time. She had been calling Troy to come home all that afternoon until that evening. Finally Troy was dropped off to their apartment complex and Kassie waited for him to come in the door as she looked out of the window. But Troy never approached the door and instead he walked to another apartment in the complex.

Kassie knew that Troy had either gone in one of two apartments. Kassie knew that an older man lived in the last apartment and a young woman lived in the other apartment. Kassie was hoping that Troy went into the older man's apartment because she knew that Troy would visit the man from time to time. After waiting for about 20 minutes, Kassie decided to find Troy.

Kassie put Kevin in his crib, locked the apartment up and walked to the older man's house. The old man answered the door and Kassie asked him if Troy was there. The man said that Troy had not been there. The man even let Kassie come inside his apartment to prove to her that Troy was not inside. Kassie knew then that Troy was at the woman's house next door.

Kassie knocked on the woman's door and Troy answered. When Troy saw Kassie standing to the door, he shut the door in her face. When Troy opened the door again, Kassie pulled out a knife and started swinging it trying to stab Troy. He ran right past Kassie and she couldn't catch him because she was very much pregnant and there was snow and ice on the ground.

Kassie had put herself in a dangerous position because she almost slipped and fell while trying to run behind Troy. She realized how stupid she looked chasing after a man who was obviously cheating on her. The adrenaline was flowing so rapid in Kassie that all she could think about was, "I'm about to have his second son and he still don't appreciate or respect me enough to be faithful."

Kassie was so angry and hurt, she walked back to her apartment and checked on her son in the crib. Kevin was sound asleep. Then, Kassie grabbed all of Troy's clothes, shoes and hats that she had bought him and cut them up. Kassie threw all the items that she cut into a bag and took them to the woman's house. Kassie knocked on the door and told the woman, "You can have Troy and here are his belongings."

Troy didn't go back to the apartment that night, because he knew that if he went home, they would've argued all night. So Troy walked to his mom's house and stayed there for the night. The woman took Troy's clothes to his friend's house and his friend saw that the clothes had been cut. He told Troy that Kassie cut his clothes but Troy didn't believe him.

The next day was Super bowl Sunday and everyone was having a Super Bowl party to watch the game. Kassie hadn't talk to Troy since the night before, so she didn't know what he was thinking or if he knew about his clothes. But Kassie knew that once Troy saw his clothes that he would be angry and would want to retaliate.

Later that day, Troy went to the apartment with his cousin to get the rest of his things. He became irritated with Kassie because she was helping him move his things out of the apartment. Troy was hoping that Kassie would be crying and begging him to stay, but Kassie wasn't. She was too exhausted and just wanted a peace of mind. Troy left and went to his friend's house to get the bag of clothes that Kassie cut.

As soon as Troy left, Kassie called her sister, Bianca and asked her to pick her up because she knew that Troy was coming back once he saw his clothes. Bianca told Kassie that she couldn't come to pick her up right away because she was preparing for her Super Bowl party. Bianca asked Kassie, "Can you call Ebony to pick you up?" Ebony was Bianca and Lori's baby sister that their mother gave birth to. Kassidy called Ebony and told her what was going on and asked her to pick her up.

Once Kassidy hung up from Ebony, the phone rang. Kassidy answered and Troy said, "I'm going to kill you Bitch." Kassidy packed her and Kevin's belongings, secured the door and left. Kassie could tell by the sound of Troy's voice that he was serious, and she knew that he was coming back to the apartment to retaliate. Although Kassie felt threatened she didn't call the police. Kassie was too embarrassed to tell anyone about what she was going through with Troy. Kassie felt like no one would understand how she could still love someone who emotionally and physically abused her.

When Troy was angry, he would hit Kassie whether she was pregnant or not. It seemed as if Troy had no conscious or remorse of how he made Kassie feel and he got off on seeing her cry. Troy would even hit Kassie in front of Kevin and it didn't even bother him to see Kevin scream when he became scared. Kassie didn't want to be judged by no one or be told what do to with her life, so she kept the abuse a secret. Kassie felt like she was living in the twilight zone and she could see her life spinning out of control but she couldn't do anything to stop it.

Kassie wanted so badly to have a normal relationship with Troy but she knew there were some deeper issues that Troy was dealing with that she didn't know about. Kassie thought that if she gave Troy unconditional love and attention that he had been missing, that he would change and love her the way that she needed to be loved. She thought that her love could change Troy's behaviors and his heart. But Kassie had to learn about life through the lessons that it was teaching her.

When Kassie got to her sister's house and she tried to act normal as if nothing was wrong at home, and she almost pulled it off. Later that evening, all of sudden Kassie felt a knot in her stomach and she knew that something was wrong. The knot in her stomach didn't have anything to do with the baby, but Kassie's intuition had been activated

God had given Kassidy a gift of discernment at an early age, and whenever she felt a knot in the pit of her stomach she knew that God was trying to tell her something. The knot in Kassie's stomach would always let Kassie know that something had happened, was happening or was about to happen and she would feel uneasy in her spirit. Most of the time when Kassie would get this feeling, there was something wrong.

Kassie became real quiet and Bianca noticed her behavior and asked, "Kassidy, what's wrong with you? You have been very quiet." Kassie shook her head and said, "Nothing." Bianca said, "Something is wrong with you, I can tell." Kassie began to tell Bianca what happened the night before and she informed her that Troy moved out. Kassie also informed her that Troy called her earlier that day and threatened her.

Kassie then shared with her how she was feeling and she told her that she was worried that Troy had been in her home. Kassie knew that Troy had retaliated and done something to her home and belongings. When Troy got upset, he always got even with Kassie. Bianca said, "Call your neighbor's and ask them to check your apartment to see if the doors are still locked."

Kassidy called one of her neighbors and asked him to check her apartment. Her neighbor checked the apartment and called Kassie to inform her that her door had been kicked in. He also informed Kassie that her clothes were laying in living room cut into pieces, her television was shattered, microwave was broken and the cord was cut. Troy destroyed everything that he could get his hands on.

At that time, Troy name had been taken off of the lease because he was no longer providing financially for the household. Kassie had been taken care of the bills all by herself. Troy knew that Kassie would be hurt by the things that he destroyed because she had bought them with her hard working money. Troy's motto was "An eye for an eye."

Kassie filed a report with the police and packed some of her items so that she could stay with Bianca for about two weeks. She couldn't bear going back to that apartment like that and she needed to figure out a life possibly without Troy. Bianca helped Kassie by being there for her emotionally, which made them become really close. They would sit up all night and just talk about life. Bianca had shared her story with Kassie and it allowed Kassie to let down her guard and confide in her. Kassie didn't feel alone anymore because she felt like she had someone who understood her feelings for a man who did everything in his power to destroy her.

Bianca would leave to go to work at a nursing home, while Kassie went to school at the university. But it was very difficult for Kassie to concentrate and focus on her studies especially with everything that she had been going through. Kassie was given a leave of absence from her job because her due date with the baby was approaching soon.

Bianca came home one night and told Kassidy that she was talking to some of her colleagues about her situation. Kassie initially became upset with Bianca because she didn't want her business in the streets. Bianca said to Kassie, "I was talking to some of the girls at my job about what you're going through with Troy. One of the girls told me that she knew Troy and that he has a bad habit." Kassie responded, "Yeah, I know he smokes weed and drinks alcohol." Bianca replied, "No baby girl, I'm talking about cocaine."

Kassie was floored, and it took her a while to process the information. Kassidy only had a little knowledge about cocaine because one of her friends had informed her about the effects that it caused. But she had been witnessing the effects of cocaine all this time and didn't know it. Kassie then remembered what her friend told her, "You don't ever want to be with a man that uses cocaine because it makes them evil and mean, and they don't care who they hurt." Kassie knew that what she was hearing from her sister was true, and that she was in for the worse ride of her life. Kassie had to decide if she was willing to put up with Troy's habit and his behaviors.

Troy called Kassie at Bianca's house later that night and she questioned Troy about if the allegations of him using cocaine were true. Of course Troy denied ever using it, but Kassidy could tell that Troy was lying to her. It finally made sense to Kassie why Troy moods would change so suddenly. One minute he was the sweetest person in the world, and the next minute he was the devil from hell. Kassie knew that she had a decision to make, whether she was going to accept that fact and still be with him or leave. However, things weren't that simple.

Once Kassie received her income tax check and school refund, she went to deposit her money into her bank account. She didn't want to keep the money on hand because Troy would take her money and spend it if he knew she had any. Kassie knew that she had other obligations and she needed her money to purchase a car and buy things for her babies.

Kassie thanked Bianca for allowing her to stay with her and her family and went home. Kassie was ready to get her life back in order. When Kassie arrived home she started cleaning up and trying to get her life back to normal. As Kassie was cleaning, a knock came at the door. She opened it and Troy was standing there. He asked if he could come in and Kassie let him in. Troy apologized to Kassie for everything. Kassie apologized to Troy for cutting his clothes. Troy then admitted to using cocaine and he promised Kassie that he would never use again. Kassie wanted to believe Troy and she accepted him back into her life.

CHAPTER 13

A MOTHER'S LOVE

On the morning of February 6th, 2003, Kassie woke with sharp pains in her abdomen and lower back. She knew immediately that she was in labor. Kassie called her sister, Lori to take her to the hospital. Troy took Kevin to his mother's house and then he went to the hospital to be with Kassie. Kassie called her mom so that she could be by her side like she was at Kevin's birth.

Kassie was in labor for only five hours, when she gave birth to her second son at 11:57 am, weighing in at 8 lbs. 4 oz. Kassidy named her son Kyle. Troy was there to witness the birth of his second son and he even cut the umbilical cord. Kassie thought that since Troy witnessed the birth of their son, that it would humble him and soften his heart. But Troy wasn't affected, not even a little bit.

As a matter of fact, Troy left Kassie in the hospital the same day her and Kyle were going to be discharged. Kassie got into an argument with Troy about money. Troy knew that Kassie had deposited her money in the bank and he wanted some. Troy became furious with Kassie when she told him that she wasn't giving him any money. So Troy called a cab and left Kassie and their newborn son, Kyle in the hospital. Kassie had to find a ride home.

Kassie called her father and asked him to take them home. When Henry came to take Kassie home, Rachael was with him. Kassie and Rachael had not spoken to each other for some time now, so this made Kassie very uncomfortable to ride with them. When Kassie entered to car she said, "Hello." But Rachael didn't speak to Kassie. Once they arrived to Kassie's apartment, Henry helped Kassie take her things inside.

Henry looked at Kassie and asked, "What's wrong with you two? You used to be able to talk to each other and now yall are not even speaking to one another." Kassie responded, "Dad, I spoke to her but she didn't speak to me. What more do you want me to do? I can't do any more than that." Kassie then told her father, "You need to have this conversation with Rachael because she is the one that has a problem with me."

After the birth of Kyle, Kassidy realized the importance of getting back to school. Kassie had already missed six weeks of school and was anxious to return. The week before Kassidy was to return to school, Kevin became ill with pneumonia. Since Kevin was born premature, he was liable to getting sick with pneumonia because his lungs weren't fully developed at birth. Kassidy took Kevin to the local hospital and they immediately admitted him. Kevin's symptoms included fever, diarrhea, vomiting, dehydration and upper respiratory infection.

Kevin had been in the hospital for a few days and it looked like he wasn't getting any better. The doctors didn't seem to know how to treat Kevin, and they said that they didn't know when he would be able to go home. Kassie missed so many days of school that semester because of the six weeks that she was out for maternity leave and now her son was sick. So Kassie withdrew from the University, for the remainder of the semester. Kassie couldn't worry about school at the moment because she had more important things that she needed to focus on.

Kassie went back to the hospital to stay with Kevin. She only left Kevin alone in the room when she knew that someone would be watching him. Kyle was being watched by Troy's sister, Sherry, and Kassie would often call to check on him to see how he was doing. Kassie wasn't so worried about Troy's where about at this point, her only concern was her children.

Kevin had been in the local hospital for almost and week and it seemed like he was getting worse. Deborah called Kassie and told her to turn to the news channel. Deborah told Kassidy that there were reports in the state of Virginia about an epidemic that was taken place of children 2 years old and younger, dying. The reports stated the children that were hospitalized were suffering from the same symptoms as Kevin was suffering from. Their symptoms also included high fever, dehydration, diarrhea, vomiting and upper respiratory infection as well.

Kassidy became very concerned after watching the news but she continued to pray and tried to hold on to her faith that Kevin would pull through. Kassidy constantly called the nurses station to ask for liquids for Kevin to keep him hydrated, although he had an IV in his arm that was supposed to be doing the same thing.

One day Kassie happen to notice that the IV had slipped out of Kevin's arm and the medicine was leaking on the bed. She called the nurse and told her that Kevin's IV needed to replaced. But when the nurse went in the room she didn't replace it. The nurse took the same IV and tried to push it back in Kevin's arm and re-taped it.

Later that night another nurse went into Kevin's room to check his vitals and then there was a loud thud that came from the next room followed by screaming and crying. The nurse asked Kassie to excuse her as she ran out of the room to see what was happening. Kassie noticed a few more nurses running to the room next to Kevin in a panic. A few minutes later the nurse returned to Kevin's room and Kassie noticed that she had been crying. Kassie asked the nurse, "Are you okay?" The nurse shook her head and said, "I'm fine" and continued to check Kevin's vitals.

The next morning Kassie turned to the news channel and again they reported two more children that had died, one in Virginia and one in Elizabeth City, NC. Kassie called her mother and grandmother to ask them to pray for her son because she was very scared at this point. They prayed with Kassie and told her that everything would be alright.

Kassie's aunt was working at the hospital and she entered the room and closed the door behind her. She whispered to Kassie saying, "You need to get Kevin out of this hospital." Kassie looked at her aunt in astonishment and asked, "Why, what's wrong?" Kassie's aunt replied, "I'm telling you this because I don't want to see nothing happen to Kevin. A little boy died here last night, and he had the exact symptoms that your son has. He was in the next room to you guys." Kassie's mouth dropped as she recalled all the commotion from the night before and how everyone was crying and screaming.

Kassie told her what she remembered from the night before and her aunt informed her that the father of the boy walked in the room and found his son dead. Then the father collapsed on the floor which made the loud thud sound that Kassie heard. Then Kassie's aunt informed her that the grandmother of the child entered the room and once she saw her grandson unresponsive in the bed and her son collapsed on the floor, she screamed.

Kassie started crying uncontrollably and her aunt gave her a hug and she said, "You need to tell them you want Kevin transferred to Children's Hospital of Kings Daughter's in Virginia. This hospital is not equipped to treat him. CHKD specializes in children and they can help him better there."

Kassie called the nurse in the room and requested a transfer to

CHKD immediately. The hospital contacted CHKD and requested Kevin to be transferred to their hospital the next day. The nurses moved Kevin to a room closer to the nurse's station that night because they wanted to monitor him closely. The nurses were afraid that Kevin would not make it through the night. Kevin had become even more dehydrated and weaker. His body was so limp and he could barely keep his eyes open.

After they moved Kevin to the new room they put him under an Oxygen Tent and blew mist on him the entire night. Kassie had to sleep underneath the tent as well because Kevin was scared to sleep under it alone. Kevin was only about 15 months old at the time.

When they woke up the next morning, the paramedics from CHKD were entering the room. Kassie got out of the bed and her clothes were soaking wet. The medic from CHKD picked Kevin up out of the bed and asked, "Why in the hell is this child wet? Are you guys trying to kill him? He is not supposed to be wet especially if he has pneumonia."

Then the medic checked Kevin's vitals and his IV, and he discovered that the IV was leaking and in fact was not in his vein. Kassie told the medic that the IV had slipped out a few nights before and instead of the nurse replacing it she just attempted to push it back in. This meant that Kevin had been without IV for at least two whole days.

Kassie became enraged because she knew that they could have killed her son due to negligence. Kassie knew that it was a miracle that her son was still alive. God had heard their prayers and if Kassie hadn't constantly asked the nurses for liquids for Kevin to drink that he wouldn't have made it.

The medics transferred Kevin to the CHKD in Virginia and Troy rode with him to the hospital. Kassie needed some time to regroup from all the stress that she had been under. Kassie went to Sherry's house to spend some time with her newborn son, Kyle. It had been a while since she had seen Kyle and she needed to see him and get some bonding time. After her visit with Kyle, Kassie's sister, Bianca took her to CHKD so that she could be with Kevin.

Kassidy arrived at the hospital and when she saw Kevin, he had an IV in his neck. The nurse explained to Kassie that they attempted to put in an IV several times on the way to the hospital in different areas of Kevin's body, but they couldn't get a good vein. The IV was placed in Kevin's neck because his veins would burst due to being under the tent the night before. Kassie left the hospital to checked in to the Ronald McDonald house and to get a bite to eat.

When Kassie arrived back to the hospital to check on Kevin, he was sitting up in the crib watching television and eating a slushy. Kassie was so happy to see Kevin sitting up by himself and holding his slushy. Once Kevin started receiving proper treatment, he was back to his jolly self. Kevin stayed in the hospital for a few more days and was released.

CHAPTER 14

UNFOOLISH

Kassidy had been out of school for months now and she knew that if she didn't start back soon, she would lose her momentum. So Kassie enrolled back in school for the summer classes. She was ready to get back into the swing of things. Kassie knew that she needed her own transportation and she appreciated the people who drove her to school but it was nothing like having her own.

One day Kassie's boys had an appointment and they had to catch a cab. Kassie was holding a baby carrier for Kyle (he was 3 months old) and a car seat for Kevin (he was 16 months old), and a huge baby bag. That outing was very difficult and it frustrated Kassie. Kassie couldn't take it anymore, and that was the last straw. At that moment Kassie made a declaration, "This is the last day that I am going to ride in a cab. I have been faithful and patient and I know God is going to bless me with a car of my own."

Kassie wasn't a religious person but she was a spiritual person and she had a personal relationship with the God. Kassidy had been building a relationship with God over the years and through the life experiences that she had. Kassie was learning on God for herself and her faith was increasing. She knew how good God had been to her over the years and she could depend on him to come through for her. Kassie always remembered everything her grandmother taught her and she knew it was time to tap into her faith.

Kassie had been saving up to purchase a car and she was determined not to spend it on anything else. So a friend of Kassie's took her to look for a car one day. Kassie knew what she wanted and she wasn't settling for anything else. She wanted an black, 80s model car, with four doors. They went to a few car dealerships but Kassie didn't see anything that caught her eye. Kassie became discouraged because the cars that she saw were out of her price range and she didn't need a car payment at that time. Kassie wanted a car that she could pay cash for.

Kassie's friend said, "Don't worry Kassie, we will find you a car soon." Kassie started to pray saying, "God I need you to help me. I've depended on others for a ride to school and appointments and I don't want to have to depend on anyone for a ride anymore."

Kassie's friend wanted to stop to one more place before she took Kassie home for the day. Sometimes there were cars for sale on the Wal-Mart parking lot, so Kassie's friend decided to check there. They arrived at the parking lot and Kassie's friend started looking at the cars. Kassie stayed in the car because they had been driving all day and she was exhausted. Kassie was almost about to give up on hope until suddenly Kassie's friend took a look at the car she said, "Kassie, check this out. It's a black 1985 Nissan Maxima, it has four doors, box shaped, it has leather interior, a sunroof, and it's a stick shift 5 speed."

Kassie looked up and asked, "Really?" It was too good to be true and Kassie had to see it for herself. Kassie walked to the car and looked at the car inside and out. The price of the car was within Kassie's price range. Kassie took a mental note of the number and decided to call the owner of the car. The owner agreed to bring the car to Kassie later that night for a closer look and test drive.

Later that night the owner brought over the car and let Kassie take it for a spin. After driving the car, Kassie negotiated a price with the owner and he agreed on that price. Kassie paid for the car and it was hers. Kassie was so happy because she didn't have to ask anyone for a ride anymore. She could take her children wherever they needed to go. It felt good for Kassie to have her own vehicle. Kassie went everywhere with that car, she even taught Troy how to drive a 5 speed.

Troy never had a driver's license and he wanted to drive the car sometimes, so Kassie helped him study the DMV book and he passed the test. Then Kassie taught him what to do on the driver's test and how to complete a three point road turn so that he could pass the driving test as well. Troy passed the driving test and finally had his driver's license.

Kassie and Troy's relationship was not all bad or else she wouldn't have stayed as long as she did. When things were good between them, they were really good, but when they were bad between them, they were really bad. Troy could be very charming at times especially when he and Kassie were alone and he wasn't trying to show off or "front" in front of his friends and family. Troy loved to cook and clean. Domestic duties were Troy's forte. When Kassie would come home from work, Troy would have the house smelling good from cleaning and cooking. As a matter of fact Troy taught Kassie a few things in the kitchen.

Troy loved a clean house and was very meticulous about how he wanted the house to be. Kassie and Troy decided that he would be the "house wife" and Kassie would be the "bread winner." For a while the arrangement worked for Kassie because she was a "Go getter" and she knew how to make the money. Kassie could never see herself as a "stay at home" mom, at least not on purpose.

Kassie liked to stay busy and was determined to make it, so Kassie worked at least two jobs and went to school fulltime. She took care of her two children and Troy. Kassie continued to work at Captain D's but she got a weekend job during the summer in Nags Head, NC cleaning houses.

Kassie had that "I got to do, what I got to do" mentality to provide for her family. Kassie's initial concern was just trying to make it out of school. Kassie changed her major several times before she decided on her final major. Kassie made the final decision to change her major to Criminal Justice.

After the summer was over, Kassie started applying for other jobs. She wanted to gain experience in a more professional field other than being a cashier at Captain D's. Kassie knew that her job at Captain D's was indeed a blessing, but she knew that the potential she possessed was much greater and she wanted to reach that potential.

Kassie received a call from a local mental health agency concerning a job that she had applied for. They provided mental health services to people such as community support, and they have several group homes for children. Kassidy landed a job at one of the group homes for girls. She was excited because it was something new and different, but she continued to work at Captain D's part time as a cashier.

For the first couple of weeks, Kassie enjoyed training for the job and learning all the intervention techniques. She mainly enjoyed working with the clients and trying to show them a better way of life. Kassidy always had a heart to help others and she wanted so much to help the children at the group home to make better choices for their life.

Kassie's life became a routine involving school, work, and home with her family. Kassie would sometimes go to her home church in Tyner, but she didn't go as often as she should have. Kassie tried to maintain a personal relationship with God and she knew where her help came from. Kassie knew that it was God who kept her through everything that she had been through and she knew that he would be the one to see her though it all.

The arguments and fights didn't cease between Kassie and Troy, and sometimes Troy would pack his belongings and stay with his mom or dad. During one of Kassie and Troy's break ups, he decided to move in with his friend. Kassie and Troy continued to maintain contact with each other but they felt that they needed some space.

Troy was working at K-Mart in Nags Head, NC and sometimes Kassie would give him rides to and from work. One night Troy told Kassie that he was going to work with a friend and he didn't need Kassie to drive him. But he asked Kassie if she would pick him up in the morning. Kassie gave Troy the benefit of the doubt and she believed him.

Early the next morning about 5:00 am, Kassie got dressed and woke up her babies and got them dressed to go pick Troy up from work. It took Kassie about 1 hour and 15 minutes to get to K-Mart in Nags Head. When Kassidy arrived to Troy's job, she called the manager and asked him to inform Troy that she was waiting to pick him up. The manager told Kassie that Troy did not come to work that night before and that he had not seen him in a few days. Kassie knew that Troy had lied to her and she was upset about it. Kassidy felt like the biggest fool for believing Troy. She drove back to Elizabeth City and confronted Troy about lying and having her drive over an hour away and he didn't even go to work.

A few nights later Troy told Kassie he had to work and that he wouldn't be able to spend time with her and their boys. Kassie didn't believe Troy, and she knew that he was lying but she had no proof. Later that night, Troy's uncle called Kassie and asked where Troy was. Kassie told him that Troy said that he had to work. Troy's uncle responded, "No he's not because he just called me from a local number."

Kassie took her children and put them in the car and went over to Troy's friend's house where he was staying. Kassidy parked on the side of the house and locked to doors so the kids would remain safe. Kassidy scoped out the parking area looking for any familiar cars and then she walked to Troy's bedroom window and she heard Troy and a female talking and Kassie snapped.

Kassie walked to the front of the apartment and banged on the door and started yelling for Troy to come out. She wanted Troy to come outside and explain why yet again he was lying to her. Kassie was frustrated and couldn't understand how she could give Troy her whole heart and he just walked all over it. After about twenty minutes, Troy still hadn't come outside. So then Kassie threatened to cut everybody's tires in the apartment complex until somebody came outside.

Then suddenly, Troy was standing at the door. Kassie jumped on Troy and they started fighting. Troy called Kassidy every name in the book except a "child of God."

Apparently the female that was in the room with Troy got scared and left out the front door, and Kassie never saw who she was. Kassie walked back to her car and when she opened the door Kyle was still asleep but Kevin was awoke and he was screaming to the top of his lungs. Kassie got in the car and tried to console Kevin and she told him, "It's going to be okay. Mommy will never leave you again." At that moment Kassidy realized that Troy didn't really love her and he really didn't know how to. Kassie started her car and drove home.

That night changed Kassidy's perspective of things and she was determined that she wasn't going to play the fool anymore. She was going to live her life for her and her children. Kevin and Kyle were all that mattered to Kassie and she wanted to be a great mom to them.

Kassie had grown tired of the same old relationship with Troy week after week. The relationship had become very toxic and she wasn't sure if it was worth the heartache anymore. Kassie always tried to keep her family together because that was what she always wanted for children. But Kassie had lost herself in the process of dealing with an emotional rollercoaster ride of a relationship. She wasn't happy and hadn't been in a very long time.

Not only were there other females that Troy cheated on Kassie with but he also tried to alienate her from her friends and family. If anyone would come to visit Kassie, Troy would flirt with them to make Kassie jealous or pick an argument with them so they wouldn't want to come visit her anymore, and it worked.

CHAPTER 15

TWO WRONGS DON'T MAKE IT RIGHT

Kassidy's boys would stay with their Godparents every weekend in Tyner, NC. Kevin would stay with Kassie's aunt Ester and her two daughters and Kyle would stay with his Godparents Doris and Frank. Ester and Doris only stayed two houses away from each other so Kevin and Kyle were never far apart. It was good for Kassie because it gave her some time for herself and every mother needs that time alone. Kassie started enjoying life instead of staying in the house on the weekends. Kassidy and Kennedy would hang out with some of their friends or go to a party from time to time.

Kassidy continued to go to school and work at the group home and Captain D's. While working at Captain D's, Kassie met a lot of different people. On one Friday night, Kassie was working at Captain D's, and it was a couple hours before closing. Two guys walked in and ordered something to eat. Kassie took their orders and told them that they could have a seat. One of the guys in particular caught Kassie's attention and she couldn't take her eyes off of him. Kassie had seen him several times before, especially when he would come in to order his food. However, Kassie didn't know his name.

Kassie started watching him from a distance and he noticed her

121

watching him. Kassie walked by his table and started sweeping the floor and he asked her, "Excuse me, what is your name?" She responded, "Kassidy. What is your name?" He responded, "Derrick." Derrick said "Well it's nice to meet you." Then Derrick asked, "Can I have your number?" Kassie agreed and they exchanged numbers.

Kassie and Kennedy were planning to go to a party one evening when Kassie received a phone call from Derrick. Derrick informed Kassie that he was going to the same party. So Kassie told Derrick that she would meet him there. Kassie and Kennedy got ready for the party and went to the gas station to get gas. The gas station parking lot was packed full of people, everybody was either going to the same party or to the club. Kennedy insisted that she would pump the gas and encouraged Kassidy to go inside to pay. Kassie started walking towards the store when she heard somebody yell, "Oh my God!" She looked over to her right and it was Derrick.

He walked over towards Kassie and they embraced each other. All eyes were on them as they stood in the middle of the parking lot hugging and talking. Derrick offered to pay for Kassie's gas. Derrick told the guys that he was riding with that he was going to the party with Kassie. He got in the car and they drove to the party. But when they got to the party the police were already there and had shut down the party before it even started. So they decided to go to a local club. When they arrive in the club a few more of Kassie's friends arrived. Derrick bought drinks for everyone including Kassie's friends. Kassie was impressed because she always liked a man who could take charge. Kassie and Derrick danced that night and enjoyed each other's company. When they left the club Derrick said, "Follow us." Kassidy and Kennedy followed Derrick and his cousin to a hotel. When Derrick approached the car, Kassie informed him that she wasn't ready to take things to the next level and encouraged him to take things slow. This shocked Derrick because he wasn't use to females turning him down for sex.

Kassidy continued to talk to Derrick on the phone and eventually Derrick asked Kassie if he could take her out on a date, and she agreed to go. Kassie met with Derrick and he took her to Nags Head, NC. They went to a restaurant, played pool, and walked on the beach. Kassie really liked Derrick because he knew how to make her laugh, and she hadn't laughed in a long time.

Derrick seemed to be really "down to earth" and he was very easy for Kassie to talk to. At the end of the night, Derrick asked Kassie for a kiss. Even though Troy and Kassie weren't together anymore, Kassie still had feelings for Troy. Although Kassidy and Derrick were dating, it wasn't serious. They enjoyed spending time together and Derrick knew that Troy and Kassie were off and on and that she still loved him, so he didn't try to pressure her into a relationship.

Troy started calling Kassie and wanting to spend time with her and their children but Kassie's feelings were changing towards him and Troy could tell things were different. So he started showing up at Kassie's apartment unannounced. Troy wanted to be around Kassie and the children more than before. Troy was actually making an effort to keep his family. Eventually Troy moved back in with Kassie and their boys.

Once Troy returned home, Kassie didn't contact Derrick as much as before but they still texted each other from time to time. Kassie was still going to school at the university and she became more focused and determined to complete that journey. Kassie had been working at Captain D's for almost three years now and she was repeatedly asked by the general manager if she would accept the shift manager position. But Kassie turned it down every time because she knew that she wanted more. If Kassie took the position, then she would have to quit school and she wasn't going to put her future in jeopardy. Kassie used to tell her manager, "If this place shuts down for good one day, then what will I have to show for it? Nothing!" So Kassie remained a cashier.

CHAPTER 16

PERSEVERANCE THROUGH ADVERSITY

Kassie was planning to go to New York with her family. Their church was going on a shopping trip, and Kassie didn't tell Troy about the trip because she knew that he would try to stop her from going. So Kassie made arrangements for her boys to spend the weekend with their Godparents.

Kassie spent the entire day with her sister. The bus was leaving that night for New York. and Kassie and Kennedy was running late for the bus. Kassie's cousin called the apartment for Kassie and Troy answered. Kassie's cousin asked Troy, "Have the girls left for the bus yet?" Troy asked, "What bus?" Kassie's cousin responded, "The bus we are taking to New York tonight." Troy became furious with Kassidy because she didn't tell him that she was going to New York.

Kassie and Kennedy made it to the bus and they traveled to New York. When they got to the city they shopped until they dropped. Kassidy purchased some school clothes for herself, because she was always putting her children's needs before her own. So Kassie made the New York trip about her. It felt great for Kassie to get the things that she needed for a change. However she did purchase her boys something while she was there. She couldn't help herself.

As they were arriving back to Elizabeth City, Kassie became nervous and her stomach was upset. Kassie could feel that something was going to happen when she got home. When Kassie arrived to Elizabeth City, she left the items that she bought at her sister's house. Kassie knew that Troy would destroy them because he was angry that she went to New York without telling him. When Kassie got inside of the apartment, Troy seemed to be calm. He treated Kassie very nice, as if nothing was wrong. So they went to sleep.

The next morning Troy woke Kassie up by dumping water on her while she was lying in the bed. Kassie woke up gasping for air and confused because she didn't know what was going on. Troy grabbed Kassie and started fussing at her about not telling him that she was going to New York. Then Troy punched Kassidy, hitting her in the eye. Kassie stood there in shock and holding her eye. Troy stood there in shock of his own actions, and he let Kassie go. Kassie began to cry and ran downstairs to get some ice to put on her eye.

Kassie and Troy had argued and fought many times before but Troy had never punched Kassie in the face. No type of abuse is acceptable but Kassie had never had a broken bone, black eye or a busted lip from Troy. However she would get bruises and scratches from the fights that she had encountered with him. Throughout the relationship, the physical abuse was the least of Kassie's problems. She had endured more mental and emotional abuse from Troy than anything else. Deep down Kassie knew that their relationship was over. She wasn't in love with Troy anymore and she wanted out of the relationship. Kassie just didn't know how to leave.

Kassidy began completing her internship hours at the group home where she was working. Kassie was glad that she could complete her hours there; because she didn't have to work for free. It only took Kassie about three months to complete her hours for Criminal Justice because she worked 40 hours a week at the group home.

Kassie grades were improving and she made the honor roll and she even made the Dean's list a few times. Kassie was proud of herself, and her determination increased as she promised herself that she wasn't going to allow anything distract her from graduating. Kassidy was so dedicated to her education that she would leave work and go to school in her Captain D's uniform. Sometimes Kassie had to take her children to class with her because Troy would not watch them.

One time Kassie had to take Kevin and Kyle to her final exam because Troy got upset with Kassie and said that he wasn't going to watch them. This frustrated Kassie very much but she knew she had to do what she had to do. Her final exams were very important to her and she knew that she couldn't miss it. Kevin and Kyle were very active in the classroom and were disturbing the other students, so Kassie's professor instructed

Kassie to go to the next room to finish her exam.

In the last semester of school, Kassie landed a job as a mentor at another mental health agency. So Kassie gave Captain D's her two weeks' notice. However, Kassie kept her job at the group home and started working there on the weekends. Kassie worked as a mentor during the week.

As a mentor, Kassie worked with clients in their homes, schools, and in the community. Kassidy's first day as a mentor, she met with her client at the school and introduced herself to his teacher. They discussed the child's behaviors and progress in the class and the teacher informed Kassie of any issues that she was having with the child. As Kassie sat down to observe her client in the classroom setting, she couldn't help but notice the other children in the classroom.

There was one little girl in particular that stood out and caught Kassie's eye. When Kassie first looked at the little girl her stomach immediately became upset, which let her know once again that something was wrong. The more Kassie looked at the little, the more she looked like Troy, his daughter and her two boys. Troy's daughter and Kassie's boys had very strong features of their dad. Troy's daughter was nine years old at the time and this little girl was eight years old.

Kassie thought to herself, "This is crazy! This little girl can't be Troy's." But the more she tried to convince herself that it wasn't true, the more the little girl looked like Troy. Kassie was sure that she was losing her mind for real this time, because she would constantly accuse Troy of cheating or lying and most of the time she was right with her assumptions. However, Kassie was hoping this time that she was wrong.

So when Kassie got home that evening, she asked Troy "Is there a possibility that you may have another child?" Kassie told Troy about her day at the school and what happened when she saw the little girl and how it made her feel. Troy just brushed it off and responded, "No, I don't have another child." Troy never really believed in Kassie's gift of discernment but he would always wonder how she knew so much about him.

Troy thought about what Kassie said for a moment and then asked her, "If I did have another child, would you leave me?" Kassie responded, "Yes I would leave you! I wouldn't be leaving because you have another child, because that happened long before I came into the picture. But I would leave you because I've already been through so much in this relationship that I don't think that I can handle anything else. I don't know how much more I can handle."

A few days went by and Kassie still felt like there was something about the little girl at the school, so Kassie decided to get to know her a little. Kassie asked the little girl what was her name and she told Kassie. Then Kassie asked her what her parent's names were. The little girl told Kassie her parent's names and Troy's name wasn't mentioned. Kassie figured that maybe she had been mistaken. The little girl looked at Kassie in a strange manner, because she was wondering why Kassie was asking her so many questions. Kassie told the little girl that she looked familiar to her and she thought she might have known her parents.

One morning Troy asked to use Kassie truck for the day, so he took Kassie to work. As Troy was dropping Kassie off, Kassie notice the same little girl getting out of the car with her mother. Apparently the little girl was running late for school that morning, so her mom had brought her to school. Kassie turned to Troy, pointed to the woman and asked, "Do you see that woman right there, have you ever been with her?" Troy responded, "No, I've never seen her before in my life." Kassie said, "Okay." From that point on, she dropped it and planned to never bring it up again.

At this point of their relationship, Kassie had become numb to every attempt that Troy tried to hurt her. Troy would often tell Kassie that no one would ever want her because she had two children. Troy would say or do anything that he could to keep Kassie insecure. This type of manipulation worked for Troy with Kassie for many years. But after a while she began to realize her worth and she allowed everything that Troy said to her to go over her head. Kassie knew that Troy was only saying hurtful things to her because he felt like he was losing the control of Kassie that he once had. Once Troy realized that his antics wasn't slowing Kassie down or stopping her from going to school, then he decided to help her by watching the kids. It's just like the saying, "If you can't beat me then join me."

The time had finally come, and it was time for Kassie to prepare for graduation. She had to take her cap and gown pictures, pay her senior dues and order her invitations. Everyone in Kassie's family knew that she was graduating, because she had mailed them invitations. Kassie went to visit her dad and stepmom to give them their invitation for her graduation. While Kassie was visiting her dad and step mom, they informed her that they went to the university to check the list of prospective graduates to see if Kassie's name was on it.

Rachael said to Kassie, "We did not see your name listed as a prospective graduate. Therefore we don't believe that you are graduating." Kassie said, "Well I'm not sure why my name is not on the list, but I am graduating." Rachael responded, "We will see if you graduate, because I looked through it twice and we did not see your name."

Kassidy left her dad's hoe very annoyed and frustrated because they didn't believe that she was graduating. Kassie didn't get the encouragement or support from them that she was expecting. Kassie went to the university to find out why her name was not on the list of prospective graduates. She talked with her advisor and the advisor informed Kassie that it didn't matter that her name was not on the list, as long as her professors put her final grades in the computer by the due date.

So Kassie went to visit all of her professors to ensure that they were all on the same page. Kassie found out that all of her professors had submitted her grades before the deadline except for one.

Kassie asked her professor, "Why wasn't my grade submitted on time?" Kassie's professor responded, "I do not have your name on my list as prospective graduate." Kassie pleaded with her professor to post her grades and tried to convince her that she was in fact graduating, but she wouldn't budge. Kassie contacted her advisor again and told her about the situation and she called the administrative office. The administration office contacted Kassie's professor and told her to post her grade effective immediately because she was in fact a graduate. However Kassie's professor still did not post her grade before the deadline but she did post it later that evening. Kassie's grade was accepted by the administrators and she was ready to graduate.

Kassie went to graduation practice but could not be excited because she was still pondering on what her dad and stepmom said and how they weren't excited for her. Kassie sat in the gym waiting for her name to be called, and when she heard her name she was so relieved and excited. It had been confirmed, Kassidy Bell was graduating from Elizabeth City State University with a Bachelor's of Science degree in Criminal Justice.

The next day was the graduation ceremony and all of Kassie's family was there to support her. Troy, Kevin and Kyle were there to support Kassidy. Kassie's mom, dad, stepmom, all of her sisters, her aunts, uncles, and some of her cousins were there to see her graduate.

After the graduation Kassie and her family decided to go to a restaurant to celebrate her accomplishment. Troy didn't want to go with Kassie to the restaurant, so Kassie took him home. Kassie was on cloud nine and she wasn't about to let Troy or anyone ruin that day for her. Kassie went to the restaurant with her family and they helped her celebrate her accomplishment. She was grateful to God that he saw her through those four years of college, even though there were obstacles and bumps along the way.

CHAPTER 17

THE PROMISE

The Monday after graduation, Kassie went to the local Nissan car dealership and got a 2003 Ford Explorer. Kassie continued to work at the group home and as a mentor. She applied for jobs in the criminal justice field but she didn't get any offers. Kevin and Kyle continued to go away each weekend to their Godparents house and Kassie's life continued on the same routine.

One day Kassie received a phone call from Kennedy. As soon as Kassie answered the phone, Kennedy said, "Hold on someone wants to talk to you." Kassie said, "Okay." Then a guy got on the phone and said, "Hello." Once Kassie heard the voice she knew who it was. It was Derrick. Derrick had run into Kennedy at the mall and insisted that she called Kassidy immediately. Kassie gave Derrick her new number and she told him to call her sometime.

Derrick informed Kassie that he had just gotten out of a bad relationship and that he was tired of the drama. He said he wanted to be with Kassie and see where their relationship could go. Kassie and Derrick started seeing each other again and the more time they spent together the more they began to fall in love with each other.

Their relationship seemed to be different this time from before. Kassie and Derrick's relationship became stronger and they connected a deeper bond with each other. Kassie would visit Derrick almost every day and they were becoming inseparable. At first Kassie was nervous about spending so much time with Derrick and she was afraid that someone would recognize her truck and wonder why she was spending so much time with him.

Troy was hardly coming home anymore because he was so busy hanging out doing his own thing, drinking, partying and cheating. It wasn't a surprise that Kassie and Troy were growing apart and Kassie knew that their relationship was over. They were still living together, but it was as if they were living two separate lives.

One weekend, Kassie's boys went to Tyner to stay with their Godparents as usual and Kassie had to work an eight hour shift. Kassie was on her way home when she received a phone call from her mother. Deborah told Kassie that her aunt Ester was taken to the hospital by an ambulance earlier that day. Kassie asked, "Why didn't you tell me sooner?" Deborah responded, "I didn't tell you because I didn't want to upset you while you were at work."

Kassie asked her mom, "What happened?" Deborah responded, "All I know is that she was having trouble breathing, so they rushed her to the emergency room." Kassie started crying and became very upset. Ester was like a second mother to Kassie and she loved her very much. Often times Kassie would call Ester for advice or just to have someone to talk to. Ester never judged Kassie and was always supportive of her.

When Kassie arrived at her apartment, she opened the door and ran upstairs to her room with tears streaming down her face. Troy was downstairs entertaining a few of his friends when Kassie entered the house. Troy notice Kassie was crying and asked his company to leave. Troy ran upstairs and asked Kassie, "What's wrong?" Kassie told him what happened to her Aunt Ester and that she was in the hospital and Troy became upset as well.

Troy was very fond of Ester and the news really affected him. They went to Tyner that night to pick up the boys because they were there for the weekend. Kassie felt like the boys would have been in the way because Ester's daughter were in the hospital with their mom. Doris and Frank was watching Kevin and Kyle once Ester was taken to the hospital. Kassie didn't want to put too much strain on Doris and Frank so she took the boys home.

The doctors transported Ester to the hospital in Greenville, NC to better care for her. Kassie prayed for her every day and asked God to bring her back to them. The hospital put Ester in a medically induced coma and she was comatose for almost a month. When Ester regained consciousness, her daughters called everyone and informed them of the great news. Kassie was so happy and she thanked God for blessing her

Ester was released from the hospital about a week later and she went home. Ester had been home for about a week, when she called Kassie one Friday morning. Kassie was on her way to work when she received the phone call from her Aunt Ester. Ester asked Kassie if she could pick up Kevin and keep him for the weekend and Kassie agreed.

Then Ester asked Kassie, "Do you have time to talk?" Kassie responded, "Yes ma'am! What's wrong?" Ester stated, "Nothing! I was just hoping I could talk to you about something." Kassie said, "Sure! I have time to talk." Ester said, "I want you to hear me out and please don't get mad at me." Kassie said, "I won't auntie, I promise!"

Ester continued, "I don't how to say this because I don't want you to get mad at me." Kassie reiterated, "Aunt Ester, say what's on your mind. Whatever you tell me, I will not get upset." Ester said, "I had a dream a few nights ago, and in my dream I saw Troy killing you. Don't get me wrong, I like Troy but I know that he mistreats you. You need to get out of that relationship, because I've seen him killing you in my dream. You are a smart and beautiful young lady with two beautiful boys, you don't deserve to be treated like that." Ester continued, "I love you and I don't want to see anything happen to you." Kassie responded, "Thank you, Aunt Ester! I love you too."

As Kassie listened to her Aunt Ester talking, she began to weep like a baby. Kassie didn't get mad at Ester, how could she? Especially when she knew what Ester was telling her was the truth. Kassie also knew that the dream that Ester had was really a vision given to her from God as a warning for Kassie. Kassie did not take what Ester said lightly. Before Kassie hung up from Ester, Kassie promised her that she would get out of the relationship before anything like that happened.

They told each other goodbye, but little did Kassie know that it would be the last time that she would ever talk to her Aunt Ester again. Kassie dried her eyes, wiped her face and went to work.

That evening Ester's daughter's brought her to pick up the boys to take them to Tyner. Kevin stayed with Ester and her daughters that night and Kyle stayed with Doris and Frank. Early the next morning Ester woke up and began having trouble breathing again, so the ambulance rushed her to the hospital. Ester started having multiple seizures which caused her brain to shut down and she became unconscious again.

The hospital admitted Ester and she was place on life support. Ester stayed in the hospital for three weeks until they took her off of life support. Ester died November 13, 2006 at 1:26 pm. Everyone was heartbroken at her funeral and it was full of friends and family who loved Ester dearly. Troy even came to the funeral because he really liked Ester and her death affected him tremendously. Kassie's heart was broken, for she loves Ester dearly and she was missing her presence.

Thanksgiving was one of Kassie's favorite holidays because her family would always get together to eat, fellowship and enjoy one another. Usually Kassie would take Troy and their boys to her grandmother's house for Thanksgiving, and that year wasn't going to be any different.

They went to Kassie's grandmother's house but Troy was reluctant about going. Troy argued with Kassie the entire ride to Kassie's grandmothers' house. Once they arrived, Kassie tried to enjoy her time with her family but it was very difficult to do because Troy was ready to go as soon as they got there. Troy stayed in the car while Kassie and the kids were having Thanksgiving dinner. After a while, Troy came inside and made a scene in front of Kassie's family and demanded that they leave. Kassie's was furious and her family told her to make Troy wait. Kassie told her family, "Don't worry, this will be the last holiday that I will be with him" and it was.

Christmas was approaching and Kassie and Troy were spending a lot of time apart. Troy did his own thing and Kassie did hers. By this time, Kassie and Derrick were spending more time together and becoming even closer. They hated it when they were apart from each other. One day Derrick called Kassie and said, "I'm ready to make our relationship official, so you need to make a decision between Troy and I." Kassie responded, "I want to be with you too, but I'm not sure how to break things off with Troy."

It was Christmas Eve and Kassie needed to finish her Christmas shopping for her boys. Kassie decided to go shopping in Virginia with her sister's Bianca and Kennedy. Kennedy drove Kassidy's truck so that they would have enough room to put their bags in. Kassie took Kevin and Kyle to stay at their grandmother's house while she was shopping for them. Troy called Kassie constantly throughout the day trying to start an argument with her about every little thing. Derrick also called Kassie and they talked throughout the day as well.

After they completed their shopping, Kassie and her sister's arrived back to Elizabeth City and went to the local mall. While they were in the mall, they saw Derrick's family and Kassie walked over and started talking to them. While Kassie was talking to Derrick's family, Derrick called her. He asked her where she was. Kassie told him that she was at the mall talking to his family. Kassie was only talking to Derrick for a few minutes when Derrick's mom said, "Look who's behind you." Kassie turned around and Derrick was standing right behind her.

Kassie liked that attention that she got from Derrick. If he called Kassie and asked where she was, he would show up where ever she would be. To Kassie's sisters, Derrick seemed creepy and somewhat of a stalker, but Kassie thought it was cute and really sweet. Derrick asked Kassie if she would spend the night with him that night and she agreed.

Kassie decided to wrap her gifts at Bianca's house, but she wanted to stopped by her apartment to get some overnight clothes. When Kassie got home, Troy was waiting for her. Kassie could tell that Troy was under the influence because she could see it in his eyes. When Troy was high, he was mean and very aggressive.

Once Kassie entered the apartment, Troy asked, "What are you doing?" Kassie pretended that she had to use the bathroom because she couldn't get her clothes because that would have made Troy suspicious. After using the bathroom, Kassie walked downstairs to leave and Troy asked, "Now, where in the hell do you think you are going?" Kassie told him, "I have to take my sister's home and then I'm wrapping presents at Bianca's house." Troy said, "Okay, when you get back I will be gone."

Kassie left and they went to Bianca's house to wrap the gifts that she had bought for her children. Kassie's other two sister's Quanah and Lori came over to Bianca's house as well. When the Bell sister's got together, they always had a great time laughing and joking. Bianca informed Lori and Quanah about the events of the day and how Kassie had a "stalker." Bianca thought it was strange for Derrick to appear at the mall where Kassie was, but Kassie didn't see it that way at all.

Quanah asked Kassie about her and Derrick's relationship. Kassie told her how they started talking again and that they wanted to make their relationship more official. Quanah asked Kassie, "What about Troy?" Kassie responded, "I don't know how to end it, but I know that our relationship have been over for some time now." Quanah told Kassie, "You shouldn't open that door, until you have closed the first one." Kassie agreed with Quanah, and she knew that she had to do something about her situation and soon. Kassie had been trying to avoid all of the drama that it could cause with Troy, but she knew that something needed to be done.

After Kassie finished wrapping the gifts, she visited Derrick. They talked for hours and Derrick stressed the idea that he wanted to be with Kassie. Kassie told Derrick that she wanted to be with him as well, and that she was going to figure it out. Kassie spent some quality time with Derrick and fell asleep. Kassie woke up about an hour later and she knew that she needed to go home. All Kassie could think about was how she was going to get out of her relationship with Troy, and she knew it was not going to be easy. Kassie left Derrick and went home.

When Kassie got home, she unlocked the door and tried to walk in but Troy had blocked the door with a chair. Kassie knocked on the door several times before Troy opened it. He finally opened the door and as Kassie walked in Troy slammed the door on her, causing the door to hit her in the shoulder.

Kassie could tell that Troy was very angry and that he had been drinking and getting high. Kassie and Troy started arguing as they walked up the stairs. Troy told Kassie, "You should have stayed where you were." Kassie tried to avoid any altercation with him so she prepared for bed.

Troy followed Kassie into the room and said, "You won't be getting any sleep tonight." Kassie asked Troy, "Why won't you just leave me alone?" Troy started calling Kassie every name in the book such as "whore, slut, tramp, and bitch."

Then Troy pushed Kassie and Kassie pushed Troy back. Kassie said to Troy, "I don't love you anymore and I don't want to be with you." Troy looked at Kassie in astonishment and asked, "Oh really? You don't love me no more?" Kassie said, "No, I don't." Troy raised his hand and smacked Kassie in her face.

Kassie became angry and her first instinct was to fight back. But she thought about what her Aunt Ester told her about her dream and she walked away. Since Troy was under the influence of cocaine and alcohol, Kassie knew that she would not win that fight. The conversation that Kassie had with her Aunt Ester was very clear to Kassie and she immediately became concerned and she started praying to God. Kassie prayed, "Lord, if you get me out of here safely, I promise I won't go back to him again."

Troy was so belligerent, and Kassie decided to play reverse psychology on him in order to get out of the house. Kassie started crying and she asked Troy, "Why do you keep hurting me like this? Love is not supposed to hurt." Troy facial expression changed because he was expecting Kassie to fight back. Troy looked at Kassie with a smirk on his face as if he enjoyed watching Kassie cry.

Kassie then said, "Let me go and get some fresh air, and I will get you some cigarettes so we calmly talk about us." Troy responded, "Yea go get my cigarettes and when you get back, I'm leaving." Kassie tried to convince Troy that she wanted their family to work and begged him not to leave. As Kassie pleaded with Troy, she was gathering her pocketbook, cellphone and shoes. Kassie walked downstairs and Troy followed her still arguing with her and Kassie pretended to care.

Once they got outside, Kassie locked the door and Troy continued to argue. Troy told Kassie that he didn't need her. So Kassie said, "Since you don't need me, then give me my keys." Troy threw the keys to Kassie and said, "I don't need your keys because if I want to get in the apartment, all I have to do is kick the door in like I did before." Once Kassie got the keys from Troy she walked to her truck and left. Kassie drove to the magistrate's office at 2:00 in the morning.

On the way to the magistrate's office, Kassie began to talk to God and she said, "I made you and my aunt Ester a promise and I will honor that promise of not going back to this man who has abused me for the last 5 years." Kassie began to cry and thank God that she made it out alive. She realized just how blessed she was because she knew that he could have killed her if she fought Troy back. God had spared her life once again and she felt obligated to him.

Kassie filed a police report and called her mother to inform her of what happened. Deborah suggested to Kassie that she should pick her boys up from their grandmother's house, and ask Bianca if she could spend the night at her house. Deborah knew that if Kassie went back home, Troy would come back.

So Kassie called Bianca and she said that it would be fine. Kassie asked the officer if he could escort her to pick up her children from their grandmothers house. Kassie went to Troy's mother's house to get the boys and Troy's mother got upset with Kassie because she had the police with her. Although Troy was an adult, his mother still considered him as her baby and she would defend him no matter what.

The officer then escorted Kassie to her apartment to get some items so that she could spend the night with her sister. When they were leaving the complex, Kassie noticed Troy walking back to the apartment. Kassie flagged the officer and informed him that he had just passed Troy walking. The officer turned his car around and arrested Troy.

Kassie was so relieved because she knew that she wasn't going to take him back and she realized that the abuse that she had to endure for the last 5 ½ years was now over. She felt a great deal of peace that came over her in that instant and that was something that she hadn't felt in a very long time.

Kevin and Kyle were in the backseat, Kyle was asleep but Kevin was awoke and he saw the entire incident. Kevin asked Kassie, "Mommy what's wrong with daddy?" Kassie told Kevin, "Your daddy hit me, so the police have to take him to jail." Kevin then responded, "Then he should go to jail, mommy." Kassie never wanted to lie to her children about anything no matter how young they were. She always wanted to tell them the truth in a way that they could understand. Kassie never bashed their father to them, but she always "kept it real" and never sugar coated anything. Kassie needed her boys to know the reason why their father was not going to be living with them anymore.

Kevin was around most of the time to witness the abuse from his father to his mother. Troy didn't care if the boys witnessed their fights or not. He would argue and fight right in front of Kevin and Kyle. Sometimes Kevin would get between his mother and father and say to Troy, "Daddy, leave my mommy alone." It hurt Kassie to know that Kevin had witnessed a lot of violence and abuse and she felt guilty for putting her children through something like that. No child should ever have to witness something like that, ever.

That was end of Kassie and Troy's relationship as a couple. It's true what they say about an abusive relationship, when the abuser apologizes and say it won't happen again, most of the time it does. An abusive relationship does not getter better, it only gets worse, unless God intervenes and changes that person's heart. If that doesn't happen, then it's a possibility that the man you love so much, could end your life.

Although Troy was arrested and taken into custody, Kassie still stayed at her sister's house that night with her boys.

CHAPTER 18

THREE FOR THE HOLY GHOST

The next morning Derrick called and asked Kassie if she was okay. Kassie told him what happened with her and Troy and Derrick decided to visit Kassie at Bianca's house. Derrick told Kassie that everything was going to be okay now.

Derrick spent Christmas day with Kassie and her family in Tyner. Everyone kept telling Kassie how happy she looked and that they made a great couple. It seemed as if Kassie and Derrick were a match made in heaven. Derrick was attentive to Kassie's needs and her boys adored him. Derrick played with Kassie's boys and gave them a lot of attention. That really took Kassie's attention and drew her closer to Derrick.

The key to Kassie's heart were her children and Derrick was playing a very important role on her boys life. Derrick even went to church with Kassie a few times. Kassie was so sure that she had found the man of her dreams. They did everything together such as going to the movies, bowling, dining out at many restaurants. One of Kassie's favorite things to do was play pool, which was something that they would do every day at a local bar.

One day Kassie came home from work and her neighbor was sitting outside and she seemed upset. Kassie asked her what was wrong and her neighbor informed her that Troy had broken into their home earlier that day. Kassie was shocked of Troy's boldness and disrespect for others because her neighbors were supposed to be his friends. Troy use to spend a lot of time at their apartment before him and Kassie parted ways. This let Kassie know that Troy's drug habit was getting out of control.

Kassie asked, "What in the world? How could he do this to you?" The neighbor responded, "We know it was him because when he used to come over here, he knew where we kept our money and he knew where to find it." Nobody ever assumed that Troy was plotting to rob them, although he robbed other people before.

Kassie's neighbor called the police and filed a report. Kassie began to think, "Wonder if I was home when it happened? He could have broken into my home too." All kinds of thoughts were running in Kassie's head. When Kassie informed Derrick about what Troy did to her neighbors, he asked if it was okay if he moved in with Kassie and the boys to keep them safe. Kassie thought it was a great idea and agreed because she didn't want to be alone.

Bianca and Lori had planned a Valentine's retreat for 4 days and 3 nights in February, it was for couples only. Kassie asked Derrick if he wanted to go to the retreat and he said yes. So they paid for their room and their portion of the groceries. Kassie was excited because she knew that they would have a great time.

Derrick wasn't working at the time and didn't have a car so they had to share Kassie's Ford Explorer. Derrick didn't have his license either because they had been revoked because of a ticket he had received previously. Kassie told Derrick since he was planning to be with her that she would help him get on his feet.

Derrick saw a car that he liked and he wanted it really bad. The car was a 1992 Buick, Roadmaster it was two toned with candy apple red on the top half of the car and smoked grey on the bottom. Derrick took Kassie to the dealership to look at the car. Kassie liked it and she told him that she thought he'd look good in it. So Kassie bought the car for Derrick to drive because she knew he was planning to get a job soon. The title of the car was in Kassie's name and she also added the car to her insurance.

Kassie's cousin worked at a lumber yard in Gatesville, NC, and Kassie asked her cousin to put in a good word for Derrick. Kassie helped Derrick fill out his application and created him a resume. Kassie took him to the interview and he got the job. At the time Kassie didn't mind helping Derrick get on his feet because she always had a big heart and she figured, "If Derrick is going to be with me, then he has to make some money to help me with the bills."

But what Kassie didn't realize was that she was handicapping Derrick as a man. Kassie wasn't allowing him to be the man and stand on his own two feet, and Derrick took advantage of it.

The week before Kassie left for the retreat, they gave Kyle a birthday party. After the party they started packing for the retreat. Kassie and Derrick went grocery shopping with Bianca and Lori for the retreat. While they were in the store Derrick's ex-girlfriend kept calling and texting his phone. Derrick claimed that she had been harassing him all day and that he told her to leave him alone. Kassie asked Derrick if he was still communicating with her behind her back and she asked him to be honest about it. Derrick responded, "No, I don't want to be with her anymore and I want her to leave me alone."

Kennedy was working at a hair salon in Wal-Mart at the time and while shopping Kassie, Derrick, Bianca and Lori visited her for a few minutes. Derrick received several phone calls from his ex-girlfriend while they were talking to Kennedy and they informed her of what was going on. Kennedy said, "When I get off, I might come over to check on yall."

After they left the shopping center they went home. Ten minutes later, Derrick received another phone call from his ex-girlfriend. She told him that she was outside, and that she wanted him to come outside to talk to her. Derrick told her, "No."

Then Kassie's received a phone call from her neighbor, and he told Kassie, "There is a girl outside and she threw something on your car." Derrick told Kassie, "Call the police." Kassie called the police and told them what was going on.

When the police arrived, Derrick's ex-girlfriend and her cousin were still there and the police talked to them and filed a report. Apparently Derrick's ex-girlfriend called her family because when Kassie looked outside again two or three cars pulled up and about seven people got out of the car.

So Kassie made a phone call to Lori and asked her to come to her apartment because she had to call the police. Lori was on her way home and she turned her car around to go to Kassie's apartment. Lori called Bianca and said, "Put your shoes back on and meet me at Kassie's house now, something has happened." When Kassie walked outside, all three of her sisters were driving in the complex, one behind the other. Lori, Bianca and Kennedy got out their cars to see what was going on. They couldn't compose themselves because they were trying to figure out what happened and why was Derrick's ex-girlfriend causing so much drama.

Derrick called his parents and they took Kassie and Derrick to the police department to press charges. On their way there Kassie became ill, she felt nauseated and she started gagging. Kassie thought that it was from the all the excitement of the night, so she just brushed it off.

A few days later Kassie and Derrick finished packing for the retreat and they were ready to go, except Derrick had to go to court early that Friday morning. Derrick still didn't have his driver's license because of a traffic violation. So Kassie went with Derrick to court and paid the money that he owed so that he could get his license reinstated.

Once Derrick's court case was over, they left and went to Nags Head for the Valentine's couples retreat. There were ten couples that were staying at the retreat that weekend. Six of the couples were from North Carolina and four couples came from Virginia. Kassie's boys were staying in Tyner for the weekend with their Godparents.

That weekend was one of the best times Kassie ever had in her life. The cottage that they rented for the weekend was a four story house with an elevator, theater, game room with a pool table, ten bedrooms and eleven bathrooms. The couples cooked, went shopping, played pool, cards, danced, watched movies, partied and had a great time. Everyone enjoyed themselves without any drama.

Kassie called and checked on the Kyle and Kevin a few times while she was at the retreat, but the boys were being well taken care of. Kassie was on cloud nine because she felt happy to be with someone who enjoyed the things that she did. Kassie felt like she had finally found the man for her and a father figure for her boys. Everyone would constantly tell Kassie that they looked good together. The couples stayed at the cottage for four days and three nights. Everyone left to go home that Monday evening.

On their way home, Derrick and Kassie didn't talk much. In fact they hardly talked to each other at all. They knew that they were back to reality and that the fantasy world that they had been living for the last few days were over. Kassie didn't want to come back home because she was remembering the events that took place before they left for the retreat. She knew that eventually they were going to have to deal with what was really going on with Derrick and his ex-girlfriend and this scared her. Kassie knew that her relationship with Derrick would never be the same.

Derrick started working at his job in Gatesville and Kassie continued to work at her two jobs the group home and at the mentor agency. Derrick, Kassie and her boys spent a lot of time together with Derrick's family. Derrick's father and mother loved Kassie dearly and they treated her and her children as if they were a part of their family. Derrick's parents talked to Derrick and Kassidy about them getting married and having children of their own.

Derrick asked Kassie if she wanted to have another baby and Kassie said, "Yes someday, but I want to be married first. I don't want to have another child out of wedlock." So Derrick started talking about marriage and buying a house with Kassie. Derrick would say all the right things that he knew Kassie wanted to hear.

One day Derrick took Kassie to look at marginal homes. They also went to car dealerships looking for a family vehicle. Derrick even took Kassie to a jewelry store to size her ring finger for an engagement ring. Kassie was so sure that their relationship was going somewhere and that they were going to be together. Kassie never dreamed that things would ever change between them.

One evening, Kassie, Derrick, Kyle, Kevin and Derrick's family went out to eat. Kassie had such as big appetite that night, she ate as if she was starving. Kassie gobbled down a double bacon cheeseburger, fries, drink and dessert. Derrick's mother and father laughed at Kassie and just kept smiling at her. A few days later, Kassie realized that her menstrual cycle was late, so she took a home pregnancy test. The test results were positive and Kassidy was pregnant.

Kassie told Derrick the news and he told his parents. But Derrick's parents didn't seem surprised at all; in fact they just smiled and said, "We already knew." Kassie asked, "How?" Derrick's mom responded, "Remember that night at the restaurant and you ate your meal like you hadn't eaten in years? We knew then."

Kassie and Derrick wanted to make sure that the test results were accurate, so they went to the women's clinic and the test results were positive there as well.

Everything began to flash before Kassidy's eyes. She remembered when she got ill on the way to the police department to file a police report on Derrick's ex-girlfriend. Kassie thought that she became ill from all of the excitement, but she then realized it was from her pregnancy. Kassie was happy about being pregnant because it was something that she and

Derrick had previously discussed and he promised to be there to help raise their child together.

Kassie, Derrick and her boys went to church together one Sunday. Derrick wanted to ask Kassie's father for her hand in marriage and to inform Henry about the news of Kassie being pregnant. Kassie's dad responded, "Well congratulations! You can have her hand in marriage and let me know the date of the wedding, let me know what you need me to do and I will be there."

Once the news circled around town, Kassie and Derrick became the talk of the town. It seemed as if everybody knew their business and everybody had an opinion about their relationship. Derrick's ex-girlfriend started texting and calling him more often and the pressure of everything became too overwhelming for Derrick and his attitude towards Kassie started to change. Derrick became distant and didn't want to be around Kassie as much as he did before. So Kassie backed off a bit to give him some space.

One morning Derrick was about to get dressed for work and he became ill. He was vomiting and he called his job and told them that he couldn't make it. Kassie took him to the hospital because she wanted to make sure it wasn't serious. The doctor asked Derrick how long he had been feeling that way, Derrick pointed to Kassie and responded, "Ever since she's been pregnant." The doctor laughed and said, "Oh, well you might be sick for a while at least." This was new for Kassie because during her other two pregnancies, she always got sick with the vomiting and nausea. The only symptoms that Kassie experienced was that she ate a lot more with this pregnancy.

Kassie had done some research and she discovered that if you have had children with the same sex, most of the time you can experience the same symptoms with each pregnancy but once the sex of the baby changes, so does the symptoms. Kassie had indeed experienced the same symptoms while she was pregnant with her boys, but this pregnancy was definitely different. Kassie was certain that she was having a girl this time, and that was what she was hoping for. Derrick already had a daughter, therefore he wanted a son.

Although Kassidy and Derrick were expecting their first child together, they continued to grow apart. Kassie really wanted their relationship to work out between them. She couldn't see herself raising three children on her own and still not married. The people in their town started gossiping about their relationship. Every week, Kassie heard something different that people were saying about her and Derrick's relationship. To add insult to injury, Kassie's own family was even talking about them. Kassie would hear all kinds or rumors such as, "Derrick is a woman abuser and he hits women, and he is going to do the same thing to you."

Kassie confronted Derrick about what people were saying about him and asked him if he ever hit a woman. Then Kassie told Derrick, "I don't care what you have done in the past with those other women, but you better not ever put your hands on me. The next man who put their hands on me like that again, will be a dead man." Derrick looked at Kassie's face and he knew that she meant every word and he responded, "I believe you too." Derrick knew that Kassidy wasn't playing with him and he knew what she had been through with Troy and that she was determined not to go through that again.

Then Kassie started hearing rumors about Derrick cheating on her and that he was still seeing his ex-girlfriend. Every time Kassidy asked Derrick if he was still seeing his ex-girlfriend, he denied it. But Kassie could tell that Derrick was keeping something from her and eventually she got tired of his games. Kassie realized that their relationship was on its way to destruction because they both were fresh out of relationships and either of them had the chance to heal and recover from them. It was doomed from the beginning. However Kassie held on to the relationship as long as she could to keep her family together.

Kassie and Derrick were only together for a very short period of time. Kassie had to go to court for pressing charges on Derrick's ex-girlfriend for attempting to damage property. Since the car was in Kassie's name, Kassie took her to court. His ex-girlfriend didn't know that the car was actually Kassie's because Derrick drove it most of the time. As a matter of fact, everyone thought that the car was Derrick's because that is what he told them, but in fact Kassie bought the car.

The morning of the court date, Kassie was preparing to leave. Derrick said to Kassie, "If she tells you that I'm still texting, calling or visiting her, she is lying." Kassie sighed and responded, "I don't want to hear it. If she tells me any of that and has proof, then I'm going to believe it because your attitude has changed towards me."

Kassie snapped and started speaking her mind to Derrick. It all felt too familiar to Kassie and she felt that Derrick was trying to cover his tracks before he got caught. Kassie was tired and she couldn't see herself dealing with the drama anymore, so she told Derrick to pack his belongings and to be gone when she got back from court.

Kassidy and Kennedy went to court and when they got home Derrick and his belongings were gone. It hurt Kassie that their relationship was over but she couldn't put herself, her boys or her unborn child through the stress of trying to keep a man that didn't want to be kept. Kassidy realized that Derrick was not ready for the life and commitment that she was ready for. In some way, Kassie was hoping that Derrick would try to fight for the relationship but he didn't. If it was that easy for Derrick to leave and not look back, then the relationship wasn't worth Kassie fighting for anyway. However it was a hard pill for Kassie to swallow, because she felt like she failed at two relationships with her children's fathers and that was never the plan for her life.

Kassidy and Derrick continued to keep in contact for a while after their breakup, until one day someone informed Kassie that Derrick was only using Kassie's friendship because he was hoping that Kassie would give him the title to the car. Derrick loved that Buick Roadmaster probably more than he loved Kassie, and it was starting to show.

Derrick thought that Kassie was so gullible that she was actually going to let him have the car that she bought so that he could drive another woman around in her car. Kassie was appalled at the fact that Derrick thought she was that stupid to let him have the car. So Kassie kept the car along with her Ford Explorer and she drove them both. One thing about Kassie, when she loved someone she showed it. Many times her love and kindness was taken for granted.

Derrick and his ex-girlfriend started dating again. A few weeks later, Derrick called Kassie because he and his girlfriend, had an argument. Derrick told Kassie that it was over between them and that he wanted to move back in and work things out with Kassie. Kassie was unsure of what to do and she talked to her stepmom, who Kassie had been spending a lot of time with lately. Kassie asked for her step-mother's opinion about what she thought she should do. Rachael told Kassie that she should go get Derrick and take him home, so she did. Kassie went to the apartment complex where Derrick was staying and took him to her place.

They spent the weekend together but they both knew that their relationship was over and that they were just going through the motions. So Derrick left that Sunday evening for good. Kassie was hoping that it would work because her boys had grown so attached to Derrick.

When Derrick left, Kevin and Kyle would cry for him. They would ask Kassie to call Derrick because they wanted to see him but he wouldn't answer the phone or respond to any of Kassie's messages. That really turned Kassie's feelings against Derrick, especially after she saw her children were hurt.

Kassie's motto was, "You can say or do what you want to me, and I'll probably forgive you and love you tomorrow. But when you hurt my children, you have crossed the line." However Kassie still tried to be cordial with Derrick because of their unborn baby.

CHAPTER 19

DEPENDING ON GOD

Kassidy promised herself that she would make the best out of this pregnancy and just enjoy being pregnant. Kassie wasn't able to enjoy her first two pregnancies because of all the stress she was going through. She knew that she had to get herself together, because now she was about to have three children instead two. Kassie broke down and began to cry out to God, and she said, "God, I need you. I can't do this alone."

Kassie started reading her bible more and praying every day asking God to keep her strong. She started going to church more, and she would even go to bible study every Wednesday night. God became Kassidy's best friend and she had to totally depend on God and his will for her life. It was amazing to Kassie that after all that she had been through, she was still able to find peace and joy. But as always, the devil was lurking around trying to steal Kassie's peace and joy.

During Kassie's pregnancy, she spent a lot of her time at her dad's house visiting with him and her stepmom. Kassie and Rachael hadn't always got along with each other and Kassie was trying to make amends to their relationship. So they spent a lot of time together talking and getting to know each other better. Kassie shared a lot of her thoughts with Rachael assuming that she had her best interest at heart. Kassie started going to her dad's house almost every day. She didn't have many people that she trusted anymore because everyone around her was talking about her and Kassie didn't want to be alone. During her visits, Kassie confided in her stepmom about many things and she begin to trust Rachael because she thought she had become her friend.

On Kassie's birthday April 10th, 2007, she received a phone call that her grandmother became sick and was taken to the hospital. So Kassie went to the hospital to see how her grandmother was doing. The waiting room was packed with most of her family in it. Kassie's grandmother had 11 children and 32 grandchildren and many great grandchildren. They were there for hours, and finally the doctor came out and informed Kassie's dad that her grandmother had stage 4 cancer. Nobody in the family knew how sick she really was.

Kassie didn't want to see her grandmother like that because she was always such a strong woman. Everyone was encouraging Kassie to spend time with her grandmother because they didn't know how much time they had left to spend with her. Kassie wanted to remember her grandmother the way that she was, a strong, God fearing woman that loved to sing to the glory of God. A week later, Kassie's grandmother died. Everybody came together the week of her funeral, and it was good for Kassie to be with her family at that time. After the funeral, Kassie's cousin who was a minister, wanted to talk to her. As he began to talk to Kassie, he revealed some things to Kassie that God had showed him in a dream that he had. He told Kassie that the night before he had a dream about her grandmother and their family. He also told Kassie, "God had his hands over your life. That is why you go through so much, because God is using your trials to push you to your destiny." At the time Kassie didn't really understand what her cousin was saying to her and what exactly God wanted her to know. But she didn't take what her cousin said lightly and continued to pray and asked God to reveal to her what he wanted her to do.

That same day of the funeral, Rachael knew that Kassie and Derrick were no longer in a relationship and were having issues. Rachael was mad with Kassie because she wasn't visiting them and wasn't confiding in Racheal as much as she did before. So Rachael went to Derrick's parents' house and tried to start confusion between Kassie and them.

One day Kassie was visiting with Derrick's parents and they informed Kassie of what her step mother said. Derrick's parents said that they knew that she was trying to cause controversy But at least Kassie knew who really had her back and who didn't. There were only a few people that Kassie could talk to and she didn't trust too many people.

Not only did Kassie continue to work two jobs during her pregnancy but she also braided hair as well. One day Troy's cousin asked Kassie to braid her hair. Even though Kassie and Troy weren't together anymore, Kassie still communicated with Troy and his family. As Kassie was braiding Troy's cousin's hair, she informed Kassie that Troy had another daughter. Kassie responded, "I didn't know that. I will make sure I tell Troy congratulations on his new baby."

The next time Troy called Kassie, she congratulated him on his new daughter. Troy said, "Thanks, I just found out not too long ago myself." Kassie asked, "How old is your daughter?" Troy said, "She is eight years old." Kassie responded, "Oh Wow! I thought you had a new baby. Well what's her name?" Troy informed Kassie of his daughter's name and Kassie realized that it was the same little girl at the school that Kassie had mentioned to Troy about previously. Kassie responded, "Oh my God, you lied to me! I knew it! I knew that was your daughter. I could just feel it. She looks just like you and you lied about it." Troy said, "I know and I'm sorry." Once again Kassie's discernment was right.

Although Kassie was still recovering from her previous relationships and she still had a long way to go, she tried to keep a smile on her face to cover up the pain. She continued to go her dad's family church, although she always felt like she was the topic of discussion every time she went to church. Everyone at the church were family and everyone knew everybody's business, even the pastor. The pastor would preach in the pulpit and he would say, "Some of you need to focus on God instead of worrying about that no good nigga."

Kassie would just shake her head and roll her eyes because she felt like the message was aimed at her most of the time. Kassie knew that the pastor was talking about her because she had confided in him several times about her relationship with Derrick. She assumed since he was a pastor that he would keep their conversation confident, instead of preaching a sermon about her. She was already going through enough being criticized by people in the community; Kassie shouldn't have had to deal with criticism in the church as well. Kassie always saw church as a safe haven, a place where you can go and be encouraged instead of being judged.

A few months had gone by and Kassie had been in hibernation from everybody. Kassie didn't want to be bothered by anyone and she felt like she couldn't trust anybody anymore. So she just stayed to herself and her children. Kassie had stopped talking to everyone in her family because everyone had an opinion about her life and how she should live it. She had even had disagreements with Troy and Derrick and she was angry with them also.

Kassie had shut everyone out of her life, because she felt that it was the only way to protect herself. Kassie was angry with a lot of people because she had put her trust in them and they disappointed her. Kassidy felt alone most of the time, and the only person that she could talk to was God. Kassie continued to go to church and she asked God to help her to get through her issues.

One Sunday at church a minister spoke on forgiveness and it seemed like forgiveness was the topic in every service that she would attend. Kassie felt like God was trying to tell her something. She thought, "How can I forgive these people when they have hurt me so bad?" But God was working on Kassie's heart slowly but surely. Kassie was determined that she wasn't going to allow what other's thought about her life effect how she lived her life. Kassie was an adult and she was taking care of herself and her two children with God's help. Kassie learned that she couldn't depend on anybody else but God.

As God started to heal Kassie's pain, she allowed some of her family members back into her life, one at a time. But it wasn't easy and it took some time because Kassie wanted to make sure that her family knew that she was not going to let anyone dictate to her how to live her life. However Kassie was finally making amends with her loved ones and it felt good. Their relationships weren't 100% but they were making progress.

One day Kassie was sitting in her apartment and she was talking to God. Kassie said, "God, I want to thank you for doing great things in me and amending my relationships with everyone. I'm talking to my family again and I have finally forgiven everyone. I'm doing great!" Kassie was so certain that she had it all together, dotting every "I" and crossing every "T". Until God spoke to Kassie and said, "No, you have not forgiven everyone."

Kassie's conversations with God were as if he was sitting right next to her, and she always hearkened to the voice of God. Kassie responded, "God tell me who I have not forgiven, and I promise that I will make it right" Then God showed her Troy's face and reminded her of all the times Troy called Kassie and she treated him like dirt.

Regardless of what Troy had done to hurt Kassie, she knew that she couldn't hold on to a grudge any longer and that she had to forgive him. The next time Troy called Kassie, she made things right between them. Kassie told Troy that she forgave him and that they should remain cordial and friendly towards each other for the sake of their children. Kassie had learned that she had become bitter because she had not let go of the past hurt that Troy had caused her in their relationship. Kassie had to let it go so she that she could begin to heal from it.

Most of the time we think when we forgive someone, we are letting them off of the hook. But that's not the case at all. Forgiveness is never for the person who hurt you, but once you forgive someone you release yourself from bondage. Un-forgiveness can keep a person from moving forward with their life and getting the full blessings from God. Forgiveness gives a person peace and allows them to love the person who has wronged them. Holding a grudge only causes a person to become bitter, and once a person becomes bitter, they can become physically or mentally ill. Kassie continued to work on her relationship with God because she knew that he was the only one who she could truly depend on.

CHAPTER 20

SENT FROM HEAVEN

Kassie went to the mall in Virginia with her cousin to shop for maternity clothes.   Kassie was excited because she had never worn maternity clothes when she was pregnant with the boys. Kassie just wore big shirts and sweat pants or her regular clothes, so this was exciting for her. Kassie got a few outfits and then they got something to eat. It was a day for Kassie to escape reality for a while and have some fun.

When they got back in town, Kassie called her sister Bianca because she wanted to go to her house for a visit. Kassidy informed Bianca that she had just gotten in town from shopping with their cousin. Bianca said that she was called into work and that she wasn't home. As Kassie continued to talk to Bianca, she drove pass Bianca's job. Kassie was driving the Buick Roadmaster. Bianca was looking out of the window as Kassie passed by and instead of her asking Kassie if that was her in the car, Bianca told Kassie that she would call her back.

Bianca called her cousin and asked her, "What car did you and Kassie drive to Virginia today?" Kassie's cousin responded, "I drove my car." Bianca then asked her cousin, "Where was Kassie's two vehicles when you went to Virginia?" Her cousin responded, "Kassidy left her car and truck home." But Bianca didn't believe her cousin because she thought that Derrick had the car and that it was him that drove pass her job.

Bianca told her cousin, "I know Kassidy is still talking to Derrick and I know that was him driving the car because I saw him." Bianca was very over protective of Kassie and she didn't like the idea of Kassie and Derrick being involved. Kassie knew how Bianca felt about her involvement with Derrick, but it was her life and she had to learn for herself. Regardless of where Kassie's relationship stood with Derrick, she still longed for him to be a part of their baby's life.

After Kassie's cousin finished talking to Bianca, she called Kassie to tell her everything that Bianca said. Kassidy told her cousin that she was going to confront Bianca and let her know that she knew what she said about her. Kassie sent her sister a message and Bianca responded with a phone call. Kassie said to Bianca, "If you wanted to know who had my car, all you had to do was ask me while we were on the phone." Kassie informed Bianca that their cousin told her everything that Bianca said about her. The more Bianca tried to explain, the more Kassie became irritated with her sister. Bianca tried to justify her reasons for talking about sister behind her back. This wasn't the first time that Bianca had done this and Kassie was fed up and had enough.

The only reason Kassie drove pass Bianca's job was because she wanted to make sure that Bianca was telling her the truth. The tension between the Kassie an Bianca had been building up for some time and Kassie felt that it was the moment to let her sister know how she felt.

Kassie told Bianca that she didn't appreciate her talking about her and her situation all of the time. Kassie informed Bianca that she appreciated her concern but she needed to let her live her own life and let her learn from her own mistakes. Bianca didn't realize that by talking about Kassie, she was only pushing her sister away from her.

Kassie eventually had to turn her Ford Explorer back to the dealership because it was becoming too much to handle, especially with the new baby coming. So Kassie drove the Roadmaster which she didn't have to worry about a car payment.

Kassie had given her baby a name earlier in her pregnancy, even before the sex of the baby was confirmed. Kassie knew in her heart that she was having a girl, and the sonogram confirmed the sex of her when she went to the doctor office. She was excited that she was having a girl and Kevin and Kyle were too.

Throughout Kassie's pregnancy, Derrick's girlfriend stalked Kassie in the community. She would follow Kassie and just stare at her every time she saw her. One time Kassie had an appointment at the Department of Social Services and Derrick's girlfriend spotted Kassie's car. She waited outside of the building with a few of her friends for Kassie to walk outside. When Kassie walked outside, they just watched her walk to her car.

Kassie had already spotted Derrick's girlfriend and her friends while she was still inside and she wasn't worried at the least bit because she knew that she was covered by the blood of Jesus.

Kassie was informed by Derrick's cousin that his girlfriend said that she wanted to have a child by Derrick too so she stopped taking her birth control. Derrick's girlfriend had become jealous and felt that her relationship was threatened because of the baby that Kassie was carrying.

One night Kassie started having labor pains and she was taken to the hospital and the doctors informed her that it was false labor. The hospital kept Kassie for a few hours to monitor her and the baby's vitals. Derrick and his family were at the hospital and Kassie's family was there as well.

Apparently Derrick's girlfriend knew that Kassie was admitted in the hospital because she started calling the room, asking to speak to Derrick. Then Derrick's girlfriend arrived to the hospital and this infuriated Kassie and elevated her blood pressure. Bianca didn't make matters any better because she constantly nagged Kassie about Derrick's girlfriend being at the hospital.

Kassie didn't need to hear about Derrick's girlfriend being at the hospital because it was only upsetting her more. Kassie believed that her false labor was God's way of warning her of that's how it would be if Bianca was allowed in the labor room when she went into real labor. At that moment, Kassie made the decision that when she start to experience real labor, she wasn't going to inform anybody. She knew how serious it meant that her blood pressure was so high and she wasn't going to allow nobody to cause her any additional stress.

During Kassie's pregnancy, she had three baby showers. Kassie's maternal family in Tyner gave her a baby shower at the church and Kassie's Uncle Sam catered and decorated it for her. Kassie's paternal church family gave her a baby shower. Kassie sisters gave her a surprise baby shower and they blessed Kassie with many gifts and she was very grateful.

A few days later Kassie's grandmother Florida became really ill. Kassie's grandmother had been in the nursing home for a few years and she was suffering from Alzheimer disease and a severe staph infection. On October 13, 2007, Kassie's grandmother Florida went home to be with her heavenly father. Kassie didn't cry at the funeral because there wasn't a doubt in her mind that her grandmother was at peace and in heaven. Kassie's grandmother, Florida looked so peaceful and beautiful and she had the biggest smile on her face.

A few weeks later, Kassie's doctor scheduled her to come in at 6:00 am to have her labor induced on November 13th, 2007. Kassie's actual due date was November 14th, which was her father, Henry's birthday and Derrick's mother's birthday. Kassie prayed to God that her daughter would be born sooner so that wouldn't have to be induced.

So Kassie started packing her bags and getting the baby's clothes ready for their hospital stay. Kassie also packed her boys clothes because they were staying with Derrick's parents while she would be in the hospital. Although Kassie and Derrick were no longer together as a couple, his parents were very much involved in Kassie and her boys lives, and Kassie was grateful for that.

On the evening of November 11th 2007, Kassie went to Tyner to pick up one of her childhood friends which was like a younger sister to her. Her name was Rhonda. She was also Kyle's God sister and Doris' daughter. Kassie and Rhonda were very close. Kassie needed someone to help her with the children for a while after she had the baby, so she asked Rhonda if she could stay with her for a few weeks.

As they were leaving Rhonda's house, Kassie's cousin called her, which was her Aunt Ester's daughter. She asked Kassie, "Why didn't you stop to say hello and chat with us for a few minutes?" Kassie responded, "I apologize. I thought you guys were asleep because it was so late." Then Kassie informed her cousin that she was scheduled to be induced on November 13th at 6:00 am. Kassie's cousin responded, "That would be a great day to have your baby because that was the same day momma died last year." Kassie responded, "What?" Kassie didn't realize that date was the first anniversary of her Aunt Ester's death, and she began to weep.

Kassie wasn't crying because she was sad, but she believed that

God was giving her a sign that her baby would be blessed. After all the hell that Kassie had to endure during her pregnancy, she thought, "What better day to give birth to my daughter than on the same day that God called her Aunt Ester home?" To Kassie, it was as if God was giving her family something to look forward to instead of mourning that day. She knew that this child was indeed a great blessing from God. Kassie sons were special to her as well, but there was something significant about this pregnancy.

The next day, Kassidy gathered her boy's luggage and took them to Derrick's parents' house so they could stay with them until she had the baby. While Kassie was at Derrick's parents' house, she became tired so she took a nap. About an hour later, Kassie woke up and ate a bowl of cereal and a piece of cake. Kassie sat back down in the chair and all of a sudden she felt he baby dropped inside of her. Kassie screamed, "Whoa! That hurt!" Derrick's mother asked, "What's wrong?" Kassie responded, "I think the baby dropped."

Kassie went to the bathroom because once the baby dropped, she was pressing on her bladder. Once Kassie was in the bathroom, she began to have really bad contractions. She knew that the baby was coming soon, and she knew just how to get the ball rolling. Kassie text Rhonda while she was still in the bathroom, and told her, "I will be ready to leave when I come out." Kassie came out of the bathroom, she kissed her boys and they left.

Once Kassie and Rhonda got into the car, Kassie told Rhonda that she was in labor and that she didn't want anybody to know until she was on the way to the hospital. Kassie asked Rhonda to take her to the mall so that she could walk the baby down. Kassie had previously researched that walking helps the baby to come down in the position easier for delivery. Kassie also knew that walking helped to ease the labor pains so she walked for almost two hours until she got tired. As the pains increased, the faster Kassie walked.

Kassie received several phone calls from her family, while she was at the mall. Deborah and Kennedy kept calling Kassie to make sure that she was okay. Kassie continued to tell them that she was fine and encouraged them not to worry. Kassie didn't want to worry her family just in case it was false labor again. But the more Kassie walked the closer the labor pains were coming. Finally after two hours, Kassie sat down to catch her breath. As soon as she sat down, a sharp pain hit her stomach and her lower back. Kassie told Rhonda, "When I get up, we are going to the hospital. I think the baby is coming."

On the way to the hospital, Kassie called Kennedy and Deborah and informed them that they were on their way to the hospital. When Kassie got to the hospital, they took her to the labor room and hooked her up to the monitor. Kassie's family arrived to the hospital and Derrick and his parents came as well. There were five people in Kassie's labor room, not including the doctors. Deborah, Kennedy, Rhonda, Derrick, and his mom were all present in the labor room with Kassie.

Kassie spent almost five hours in the labor room. Derrick's girlfriend called Kassie's room several times while she was in labor. Kennedy answered the phone a few times and Derrick's mother answered and they asked her to stop calling, but she continued. This frustrated Kassie because she was in so much pain and her blood pressure was elevated and it didn't help that she could hear the conversations going on around her. Derrick's girlfriend couldn't handle the idea that Kassie was about to have his baby, and that Derrick was by Kassie's side.

Derrick stayed with Kassie for a few hours but left before she gave birth to their daughter. The pain that Kassie was going through was excruciating and her blood pressure was getting higher and higher. The nurses asked Kassie if she wanted an epidural to relieve the pain and she told them, "No. I didn't have an epidural with my boys and I don't want one with my daughter either." Kassie just wanted to get it over with.

The nurse checked Kassie's cervix and finally she was fully dilated. The nurse said, "Okay, we will be ready for you to push once the doctor gets here. Dr. Stevenson is on call tonight. Is it ok that he deliver your baby?" Kassie said, "Yes that is fine. Dr. Stevenson delivered my two sons, so I am very comfortable with him delivering my daughter as well."

Kassie was glad that she went in labor on her own because she was told that if her labor was induced, it could be even more painful.

Finally, it was time for Kassie to push and Kennedy was holding one of Kassie's legs and Rhonda was holding the other. It took several minutes for Kassie to push the baby's head out and Kennedy fainted as soon as the baby's head pop out.

So Derrick's mom continued to hold Kassie's leg up for her as she pushed. After about several contractions, Kassie's daughter was born. When the doctor showed Kassie her baby, she was the biggest baby Kassie had ever seen. Everyone in the room made a bet on how much they thought the baby weighed. Kassie said that she was probably 8 pounds or more and Derrick's mother said that the baby was about 7 pounds. The nurse took the baby and put her on the scale and everyone on the room was astonished at how much the baby weighed.

Kassie named her daughter Kourtney and she was born November 13th, 2007 at 12:03 am, weighing at 9 lbs. and 9 oz. Kourtney was born exactly a year after Kassie's aunt Ester died. Kassie knew that Kourtney was sent from Heaven as a blessing to her family so that they would celebrate life instead of mourning the death of their loved one. It's amazing how God works. His ways are not like our ways and his thoughts are greater than our thoughts. He knew that the anniversary of Kassie's Aunt Ester death would have been difficult for everyone, so he intervened and blessed the family with the gift of a child.

Kassie was so overwhelmed with joy and she couldn't believe how beautiful her daughter was. Rhonda videoed the entire birth without Kassie even knowing, but Kassie was very happy that she did. Kassie's boys wanted to meet their baby sister so they went into the room to see her and they went home after with Derrick's parents.

CHAPTER 21

ENOUGH IS ENOUGH

After Kassie gave birth to her daughter, she saw life a lot different. Kassie was determined that she was going to live her life that way that she wanted to. Kassie wasn't concerned with anyone's opinion and she didn't care what anybody thought about her. If Kassie felt that someone around her was not giving her the positive energy that she needed, she would cut them off.

Kassie cut her circle down to just a few people that she dealt with. Anyone who approached Kassie with a negative spirit, she disassociated herself from that person. Kassie didn't have time for people who only wanted to take from her instead of giving. Kassie always gave with her whole heart, whether it was her love, attention or financially. But if Kassie wasn't going to get just as much as she was given, then she wouldn't even deal with the person. Kassie felt like she had been used by many people in her life because of her kind heart. She had been selfless and always opened her heart to people, but after a while she had become cold, distant and bitter.

Kassie left her two jobs to work for another mental health agency where she was hired to work full time. At this job Kassie was a Billing

Specialist and Receptionist. Kassie wore many hats at this job and it was very demanding. Kassie completed the intakes for all the new clients and scheduled appointments and she was also the transportation coordinator. Kassie did it all and she really enjoyed the job but she was always looking for the next best thing. Kassie stayed there for about a year and then she received employment at another agency as a Case Manager, making more money.

Kassie's relationship with her daughter's father really became extinct because Derrick took her kindness for weakness. Derrick thought that because Kassie treated him nice, that he could still play his mind games with her. One morning Derrick called Kassie and propositioned her to sleep with him, but Kassie turned him down. Kassie reminded Derrick that their relationship was over and encouraged him to take more interest in his daughter and financially providing for her. This led them into a heated argument and Kassie hung up.

Derrick told his girlfriend that Kassie asked him for some money but he failed to mention that he initiated the call and asked to sleep with Kassie. Kassie was on her way to work and noticed that she was being followed by Derrick's girlfriend, so she pulled over. Kassie walked over to see what Derrick's girlfriend wanted, and she told Kassie to stop calling Derrick and asking for money. Kassie responded, "I will call Derrick anytime I need something. He is Kourtney's father." Then Kassie let her know the full conversation that her and Derrick had that morning because apparently Derrick had left important details of the story out. Kassie felt like Derrick was trying to cause friction between her and his girlfriend, so Kassie had to set her straight and let her know what was really going on.

After Kassie finished talking to Derrick's girlfriend, she went to work. Once she got to work, she put her belongings at her desk and went to the bathroom. When she came out of the bathroom, Kassie checked her phone and saw that she had a voicemail. Kassidy checked the voicemail and Derrick had left her a message. The message said, "Please stop calling and harassing me, and leave me and my girl alone before I go downtown and put a restraining order out on you." Kassie was amazed at how Derrick had to turn the blame on her because he was angry that she turned him down for sex and that she told his girlfriend everything.

Kassie thought to herself, "Did he forget that he called me?" He had convinced his girlfriend that Kassie contacted him for money instead. Derrick loved playing games with Kassie and his girlfriend. He got off on starting drama between the two of them. Kassie knew Derrick's antics all too well and she was determined that she wasn't going to fall for them anymore.

One time after they broke up Derrick asked Kassie, "Why didn't you fight for me?" Kassie was tired of making a spectacle of herself over of a man. She did that enough when she was in a relationship with Troy and she refused to give anybody else that type of energy again.

After that Kassie didn't want to deal with Derrick anymore, so she decided to put him on child support instead of asking him for help. Kassie would rather go through the child support agency than to deal with Derrick and his childish games. She even stopped visiting Derrick's parent's house, but it wasn't because she didn't like them anymore but Kassie needed her space from all of Derrick and his drama. Kassie wasn't going to fight a battle that wasn't hers to fight, she felt the relationship had been over and it just wasn't worth it.

A few months went by and Kassie received a phone call from her sister Lori. Lori called to ask Kassie if she knew that Derrick's father was in the hospital. So Kassie called Derrick's parent's house and Derrick' brother answered the phone and told Kassie that his father died that morning. Kassie couldn't believe it and she thought it was a bad joke, so she hung up the phone. She was denial and she didn't want to believe that Derrick's father was gone. Derrick's father and Kassie had a very special relationship, he was like a father to her and he treated her children with love.

Later that morning, Derrick visited Kassie and encouraged her to bring Kourtney to his mom's house. Kassie took Kourtney to see her family so that she could spend some time with them and they encouraged Kassie to stay for a while. Kassie visited them during their time of bereavement and accompanied them to the funeral as well.

Many people questioned Kassie why she spent so much time with Derrick's family. But Kassie wasn't concerned about what others thought of her or had to say about her. She felt that she didn't need to explain her reasons why. She just wanted to be there for them at that time because they always had a special bond and she knew that they were there for her. Kassie always did the opposite of what others expected her to do, she was different. She wouldn't respond to situations as others would.

Kassie was ready for a change of scenery so she decided to move into a house. She needed a new start, and the two bedroom apartment that she had been living in for the past 8 years was becoming too small for her and her family. So Kennedy helped Kassie find a house close to the local university. It was a three bedroom house, with a front yard and big back yard. It was just what Kassie needed at that time.

Kassie changed jobs again because she was trying to find what best suited her. She gained employment at another mental health company in Edenton, NC. Kassie really liked that job in the beginning, and her salary was $35,000. That was the most money that Kassie had ever made on a job, so she worked hard to keep it. Kassie was a Case Manager and she supervised at least 5 community support specialist, and monitored at least 15 clients. Kassie learned a lot about the paperwork aspect of the case management position at this job and became more hands on.

Kassie and Troy would still communicated concerning the boys from time to time and he would often call Kassie and ask to speak to Kevin and Kyle. One day Troy called Kassie to inform her that he had been arrested for breaking and entering someone's home. Troy didn't tell Kevin and Kyle that he was in jail because he didn't want them to know what he had done so he told them that he was out of town.

Before Troy had been arrested, Kevin and Kyle would spend almost every other weekend with him. Troy loved all of his children but there was a special bond between him and his boys. Troy would ask Kassie if he could keep them on the weekends to give Kassie a break. Kassie appreciated Troy for keeping the boys for her, and spending quality time with them. Troy enjoyed spending time with his boys and it meant the world to Kevin and Kyle, because they loved their father very much. Nothing in the world could replace the time that they shared together.

The morning of May 3, 2010, Kassie arrived at work. It was a Monday morning, which was the busiest day of the week at the agency. Monday's were "billing day" and Kassie had to organize all of the documents and timesheets by a certain time of the morning.

Kassie received a phone call from a friend of hers. Kassie's friend asked, "Are you okay?" Kassie responded, "Yeah, why wouldn't I be?" She said, "You must not have heard the news." Kassie asked, "What news?" Kassie's friend said, "Troy was killed in a fight last night in jail, and the guards found him dead in his bed this morning." Kassie asked shockingly, "What?" Kassie couldn't believe what she was hearing. Kassie dropped the phone and sat to her desk just staring at the wall. It was as if she was in a bad dream, but she couldn't wake herself up from it.

Then Kassie received a call from one of Troy's friends and he called to check on Kassie as well to see if she was okay. He confirmed that Troy was dead. Kassidy tried to call everyone in Troy's family that she could think of but nobody answered. Kassie called her mom and informed her of what happened to Troy and asked her to accompany her back to Elizabeth City. Kassie wanted to pick up her boys from school before they heard the news from someone else. Deborah drove Kassie back to Elizabeth City as Kassie still tried to process what happened and how she was going to tell her boys what happened to their father.

Kassidy picked up her boys from school and took them home. Once they got home, Kassie noticed Derrick pulling up in her driveway. Kassie took Kevin and Kyle in the room and locked the door. Kassie wanted to be the one to tell her children and she didn't want Derrick or anybody to be present. Kassie didn't feel that Derrick's concern for the boys was genuine at the time.

Once they were in the room, Kevin and Kyle asked, "Mommy, What's wrong?" Kassie responded, "Your father passed away this morning." It took Kevin and Kyle a minute to realize what their mom was telling them and they begin to weep. They began to question Kassie,

"Where was he? What happened? Did somebody hurt Daddy?" Kassie tried to comfort her sons the best she knew how. She tried to answer their questions as correctly as she could, but it wasn't easy. Kassie didn't really know the full story yet and she was only going by what she was told.

Kassie told her boys, "Your father was in jail for stealing something that didn't belong to him and he has been there since January. I was told that he got into a fight with an inmate and he died." Kassie tried to explained to her boys what happened to Troy the best way she possibly could. It was very difficult for Kassie to see her boys hurting this way and she encouraged Kevin and Kyle to ask questions and talk about their dad. She let them know that it was okay to cry, scream, and be angry. But she knew that the more that Kyle and Kevin released that the closer they could begin their healing process. Kassie assured her boys that she would be there to help them get through it in every way that she knew how.

Kassidy couldn't imagine the pain and the hurt that they felt. The boys were angry that Troy had lied to them about being out of town, instead of telling them that he was in jail. But Kassie understood why Troy told Kevin and Kyle that but the boys couldn't understand it at the time. Kassie would have given anything to take their pain away, but she couldn't. This was something that Kyle and Kevin had to go through and Kassie understood that there was always a reason for everything that happened in life and a lesson to be learned in it.

Although Kevin and Kyle were hurting, their strength amazed Kassie because they were determined to go to school every day that week. They didn't want to miss school, although they acted out in school a few times, but that was to be expected. Troy's funeral was full of his friends and family. The family needed someone to sing a solo at the funeral, so Kassie offered to sing for them. Kassie sung "The Battle Is the Lord's" originally by Yolanda Adams. Kassie didn't cry at the funeral because she was trying to be strong for her children. She knew that it was God who had given her the strength that she needed to get through that grieving period.

When Kassie went back to work the next week she was exhausted. She didn't realize how much of a toll that Troy's death took on her. Kassie asked her supervisor if she could take a day off, and the owner and her supervisor was very insensitive and encouraged her to stay and work the rest of her shift. Kassie realized that they were all about making money and didn't care about the emotional wellbeing of their employees. It is true what they say, "You find out who has your back, when things get real."

CHAPTER 22

SECRETS

Kassidy had enrolled in a university online for her Master's degree. She received her first refund check from the school and decided to get a new vehicle. She wanted a crossover vehicle with a third row seat, because her children were growing so fast. She went to Virginia and put money down on a 2005 Dodge Durango.

God had exceeded Kassie's expectations because she had prayed for a crossover but she was able to get something bigger. Kassie was excited about her new truck but she knew that she couldn't anyone at her job because they wouldn't have been happy for her. The people at Kassie's job were very jealous. They didn't like to see anybody else try to better themselves because they wanted to feel superior to others. They would pretend to be happy for someone, and then talk about the person when their back was turned. So Kassie continued to drive the Roadmaster to work because she knew that the people on her job would treat her different.

After about two months Kassie decided to drive her new truck to work because, she wanted to give her car a break. When she got to work, her co-workers gave her the hardest time. They asked many questions about how she got the truck, how much she paid for the truck, and where she got it from.

A few days later the agency held a meeting with Kassie and decided to give her a salary decrease. Kassie's salary was decreased from $35,000 to $24,960 because they thought that they were paying her too much money. They were like "crabs in a bucket" and instead of encouraging others to do better, they would criticize and try to hinder other from getting ahead.

They did everything that they could to get Kassie to quit. The CEO of the agency was hoping that Kassie would get angry in the meeting and quit, but Kassie remain calm and showed no emotion on her face. She refused to show them that she was really upset on the inside. The CEO asked Kassie if she had anything to say, Kassie responded, "No" with a smile on her face.

After the meeting, the CEO called one of Kassie's co-workers and asked her if she had tipped Kassie off because she didn't react to the salary decrease. Kassie was contacted by her co-worker and was informed of what her CEO said about her after the meeting. Kassie knew that her days at the agency were numbered There were a lot of unethical and under handed things that Kassie had witnessed while working at that job.

Kassie knew that they wanted her to quit instead of them having to fire her, because they had did the same thing to another employee previously.

The following week, Kassie received her first write up. She had been there a year and had never been written up before so she knew it was a part of their scheme to get her to quit. The owner fired their transportation staff, so Kassie had been their only means of transporting clients to and from appointments and she was promised a gas allowance for mileage.

When payday arrived, Kassie went to pick up her check and noticed that her salary was decreased more than what had been discussed in the meeting and she didn't received her check for gas mileage. Kassie had reached the end of her rope and she had enough. She wrote the agency a resignation letter, turned in her keys and left.

Kassidy was upset at first because she knew that she had three children at home and she needed a steady income. But Kassie also knew that God had a greater plan for her, she just wasn't sure what that plan was yet. Kassie was out of work for about three months and yet God still made a way for her and provided for her family.

Kassidy landed a job at another mental health agency in Elizabeth City. This was good for Kassie because she only lived 5 minutes from her job. But Kassie still struggled and she felt as though there was still something missing in her life. Kassie didn't stay at this job very long either and she thought to herself, "Well maybe it's me." She was dealing with the same drama at this job as the last job. Kassie tried to stay as long as she could because she knew that her family needed the money or at least she thought they did. Kassie would pray every day before she went to work and it seemed like the more she prayed the more things tumbled out of control. At the time Kassidy didn't understand what was going on.

Sometimes in life we hold on to the things that God is trying to get us to let go of, because he wants so much more for our lives. God always see's the greater potential in our lives, even when we don't see it in ourselves.

One night Kassie was working late as she did very often and one of her coworkers was working late as well. Kassie had her children in the office with her while she worked on organizing a few charts. Kassie's co-worker approached her and said, "I see and hear a lot of things that goes on around here and I don't say much about it. But I want you to know that they are plotting on you, trying to get you to quit and I don't like it."

Kassie had the feeling that she wasn't liked by her employees and she knew that they were plotting against her. She could feel the tension every time she walked in the office. They were intimidated by Kassie, not because they were afraid of her physically but because of the confidence that Kassie displayed and some people didn't like it. Kassie was shocked that her co-worker informed her about what they were plotting against her.

Once Kassie's co-worker saw her children, she knew that she had to say something to Kassie about it. Kassie's co-worker realized that they weren't only hurting Kassie, but they would be hurting three innocent children as well. Kassie worked at the agency a few more weeks and she resigned.

It had been a year since Troy had died and Kassie had never really grieved his death. She wanted to be strong for Kyle and Kevin but guilt was eating her up inside. She had been tormenting herself internally and nobody around her knew what she was going through. Kassie was feeling guilty about Troy's death, and she felt like it was her fault that he was dead. She didn't tell anyone because she thought it would sound crazy, so she kept it to herself.

While Troy was incarcerated, he wrote Kassie several letters and she never responded to the letters. However, Kassie would always accept Troy's phone calls. Kassie thought that if she wrote Troy back that it would mislead him in thinking that there was more to their relationship other than friendship. Kassie never got the chance to tell Troy why she didn't write him back.

But after Troy died, Kassie felt like if she had wrote him back that it would have gave Troy some kind of hope or something to look forward to. She felt that if Troy had something to look forward to, then he might have tried to avoid the altercation that resulted in his death.

One Sunday, Kassie went to church. Kassie was approached by her pastor and he told her that he could tell that she had been harboring feelings about something and that she needed to release it and let it go. He reminded Kassie that everything happens for a reason and that there was nothing that she could have done to prevent Troy's death.

After hearing that from her pastor, Kassie released all of those feelings of guilt and she let it go and she finally began to grieve Troy's death. It was like a weight was lifted off of Kassie's shoulders and she was able to move forward.

Since Kassie still was out of work, she started focusing on her dreams and she thought a lot about what she wanted to do in life. She knew that there was a higher purpose for her life but she didn't have a clue as to what that purpose was. So Kassie decided to drive to Atlanta, Georgia on a late Friday night to audition for Sunday's Best.

Kennedy thought Kassidy was losing her mind because she acted on impulse and decided to leave for Atlanta. Kennedy contacted their pastor and informed him of Kassie's plans to audition. Their pastor called Kassie and encouraged her not to go to the audition and tried to talk her out of it. Kassie couldn't believe her ears. She thought that if she didn't have anyone else's support, that at least she would have some support from her pastor.

Kassie's faith was working overtime and she thought that this would be the best time to follow her dreams and activate her faith. Kassie was trying to stretch her wings to see if she could fly and all she needed was support from her family and pastor. Kassie knew that there was a greater destiny for her life and she was searching for that something.

Kassie knew that thousands of people would be auditioning for Sunday's Best and she wasn't being arrogant and saying that she would be the winner. She just wanted to see how far she could go.

Kassidy left in the middle of the night with her children, her mother, her sister Kennedy and her niece and nephew. She drove all the way from Elizabeth City, NC to Savannah, Georgia. The last two hours of the trip Kassie asked Kennedy to drive because she needed some rest before she auditioned because she spent all night driving.

Once Kassie arrived to the church where the auditions took place, she saw thousands of people waiting in line. She stood in line for four hours until she finally got inside. Once Kassie got inside, she received her packet and a sticker to put on her shirt. As Kassie begin to complete her application, she started looking around at everyone. She noticed people were singing in front of the cameras trying to be noticed. Everyone was putting on a show instead of glorifying God.

Kassie got up and walked in the lobby, she asked one of the Sunday's Best staff how long did the auditions take. Kassie was informed that there were three levels of auditions that she had to pass. The lady also told Kassie, "I hope you are prepared to stay until tomorrow morning." But Kassie wasn't prepared to stay until the next morning and she realized that she hadn't really prepared for the audition at all. So she decided to leave. Kassie's family was sitting in the car for almost 6 hours and it was a hot day and they were tired. Kassie didn't audition for judges but she was still glad that she went and had the experience. Kassie still knew that she was destined for greatness but she realized that Sunday's Best wasn't a part of that destiny.

One Friday night, Kassidy went to church with her family. The spirit of the Lord was so electrifying and everyone was praising God in their own way. People were getting healed, getting prayer, being prophesized to and delivered from their afflictions. The speaker for the evening was a prophetess from Maryland. She was speaking into people lives and praying for them. She would walk the floor back and forth, holding on to the microphone and listening as God spoke to her. As she received a word from God, she would look into the person's eyes that God was speaking to her about and tell them something about their life, prophesying to them.

The prophetess then started to tell a story of a woman who had been molested, raped, abused and used. She said, "God wants this woman to know that her life is not over, but it's the beginning." She also stated that this woman had been under a "Generational Curse." Kassidy had heard that term several times previously and it had been explained to her that a generational curse was something that is passed down from generation to generation.

A generational curse is when something has happened to a parent or grandparent and then the cycle repeats itself through the next generation. Generational curses can also be an illness or behavior someone suffers from that has been passed down from one generation to the next. It can also result from something happening in a family that is kept a secret and the same patterns and behaviors continue without dealing with the issue. By keeping something a secret, it can hinder a person psychologically and emotionally resulting in physical illnesses.

So the prophet continued with her story concerning this lady, who had been molested as a young girl, raped, used and abused. As the prophetess talked, she continued to walk around the room. But this time she never looked at anyone, instead she kept her eyes on the floor as she listened to God's voice. The prophetess stated, "This woman never talks about being molested or raped. She just brushed it under the rug as if it never happened. She has kept it a secret for all of these years. The same thing happened to her mother years ago and she too kept it a secret." Kassie kept her eyes on the prophetess because she was anxious to know who this woman was that she was speaking of.

Suddenly the prophetess stopped and she turned towards Kassie while pointing and asked, "This woman that I am speaking of is you, isn't it?" Kassie's mouth dropped as tears filled her eyes and everything that the prophetess had spoken flashed before her eyes. All the memories of shame, confusion, and pain that Kassie thought that she had buried deep down inside, had resurfaced.

Kassie had been molested as a young child and she was raped when she was a teenager. She never spoke these incidents to anybody except for Kennedy. Kassie knew that she could trust Kennedy with this information and Kassie knew that Kennedy would never tell anyone. Kassidy never dealt with her issues of being raped or molested because that was something that she never wanted anyone to know about. She felt embarrassed and it made her feel as if she was weak. Kassie never like to show weakness or feel vulnerable because she felt that it gave the person who hurt her power over her emotions.

Kassie had hidden those wounds for many years and she thought if she hid it long enough that those wounds would go away. But Kassie never healed from her wounds and her life exemplified it. That was the reason why Kassie had insecurities and problems in her relationships with men. It was also the reason Kassie thought it was okay to stay in an abusive and toxic relationship with Troy, because she didn't think that she was worthy of anything more. One thing that Kassie have learned over the years is that every behavior and sickness has a root.

It's the same when you have a fleshly wound and it is kept covered up, the wound will take longer to heal because it doesn't get the air that it needs to heal and it can become infected. Therefore, the same thing happens when you have wound inside of your heart. If the wound inside your heart is kept covered up and hidden, the person can become infected mentally, emotionally and physically because it's never exposed and dealt with so that the person can begin to heal.

When a person has been molested, raped, used and abused, it's hard for that person to trust anyone or let them inside their heart. A person's heart can become very cold and bitter towards others, which can be very lonely. Kassie had allowed what she experienced to affect her relationships with men and others. It lowered her self-esteem and self-respect and often times made her insecure about what others thought of her. It also made Kassie believe that everything that happened to her, was her fault. But Kassie's secret had been exposed and that's when her healing began to take place.

CHAPTER 23

WALKING BY FAITH

Kassie registered for classes again in the summer of 2011 to complete her Master's degree, this was her third attempt. Kassie started classes on June 27, 2011 at South University online and she also started a new job at a daycare center in Elizabeth City, NC. Working at a daycare was something new for Kassie and she always liked trying new jobs to see what she was good at. Kassie started as a substitute teacher and she remained a substitute until August of that year, then they made her full time employee as a teacher assistant. It took Kassie some getting used to because she was used to making at least $12 an hour. To Kassie, the daycare was a stepping stone until she completed her Master's degree.

To continue to work at the daycare, Kassie was required to obtain her Early Childhood Credentials in order to stay employed. Kassie enrolled at the College of the Albemarle for one semester. She started in January of 2012 and completed her credentials in May of 2012. Kassie was enrolled at both schools at the same time. She completed her Masters of Science degree in Criminal Justice specializing in Public Administration from South University online on June 12, 2013. It was a real struggle for Kassie to work a full time job, attending two schools and supporting a family at the same time, but with God all things are possible and she wouldn't quit.

Kassie worked at the daycare for two years and on August 30th of 2013, the director of the daycare handed her a letter. The letter stated that the daycare would be closing at 6 pm on that day. Which meant that was Kassie's last day of work, and Kassie couldn't have been happier. She was ready for a fresh start to pursue her dreams and purpose in life. However she felt sorry for her co-workers because they didn't understand that God had a greater plan and they felt hopeless when the daycare closed. But Kassidy knew that if God closes a door, that only means he is about to open up a bigger door for her to walk through.

Over the years, Kassidy learned that the devil job is to steal, kill, and destroy. If you don't know who you are in God, you can lose focus of God and his glory. When God has a mandate on your life, everything that the devil meant for your bad, God will turn it around for your greater good.

Although Kassie had been through a lot in her life, God continued to keep her mind. If she had of taken her mind off of God, she could have easily given up and have lost her mind. Sometimes in life we have to go through so much and it seems like the easiest thing to do is to give up. But once you tap into your faith and allow God to restore you, then you too will realize that you can make it.

LETTER TO THE READERS

This book was written to show God's glory over my life and if it had not been for God and his son Jesus, I don't know where I would be. I want everyone to know that if you have been molested as a child or raped, that it is not your fault. You can get through it but you must uproot the issues that plague you and deal with it or it could cost you your life. Don't give your abuser that much power over your life by hiding it and keeping it buried in your heart. Once you dig up that root and deal with it, forgive your abuser. The forgiveness is not for them but it is for you to be released so that you can get the full blessings from God.

I also want you to know that if you have been in or are in an abusive relationship, you can make it without your abuser. If you are still in an abusive relationship, get out as soon and as safely as possible. Don't ever think that it can't happen to you or that it will get better because the abuse only gets worse. If that person is not going to therapy, getting counseling from a minister or haven't given their life to Christ, then they will not change because they can't do it on their own.

Single ladies, wait on God and let him send you the man that he has for you. God knows the plans that he has for your life better than we do, so allow him to complete you and make you whole in him and only then will God send you your Boaz.

Young parents, just because you have a child at a young age and out of wedlock doesn't mean that you can't be a good mother or father to your children. Don't allow anyone to tell you that your life is over and that you can't be successful because you have a child. Never let anything or anyone deter you from following your dreams. If you lay down to have a baby, then be woman or man enough to provide for that child even if the other parent of the child is not there to help. Don't become a statistic and put your responsibilities on others, because your children were not asked to be here.

Sometimes throughout our journey in life, we leave God. But I know today that no matter how many times we leave God, he never forsakes us. He knows our ending before our beginning.

I believe that all things are possible with God and that you can achieve anything as long as you are determined and keep the faith. What's next for my life? I'm not sure, because God is still writing those chapters of my life. But one thing is for sure, it will be something spectacular!

Jeremiah 29:11 (NKJV) – *"For I know the thoughts that I think towards you, says the Lord, thoughts of peace and not of evil, to give you a future and a hope."*

ABOUT THE AUTHOR

KENESA BOWE

Kenesa Bowe began working on this book August 14th, 2013. God gave her the vision to tell this story about her life to help other women that may have gone through or are going through the same things. This is the first book that she has written.

www.ingramcontent.com/pod-product-compliance
Lightning Source LLC
LaVergne TN
LVHW020055090426
835513LV00029B/1515